Cecilia Anne Jones

The Life of S. Elizabeth of Hungary, Duchess of Thuringia

Elibron Classics
www.elibron.com

Elibron Classics series.

© 2005 Adamant Media Corporation.

ISBN 1-4021-7800-X (paperback)
ISBN 1-4021-1156-8 (hardcover)

This Elibron Classics Replica Edition is an unabridged facsimile
of the edition published in 1873 by J. T. Hayes,
London.

Fried. Overbeck inv.

Friend. Ludy sculp.

S. Elisabeth.

THE LIFE

OF

S. ELIZABETH OF HUNGARY,

DUCHESS OF THURINGIA.

BY

C. A. JONES,

Author of "A History of the Church," "Bible History," "Church Stories,"
"The Saints of Old," "Our Childhood's Pattern," &c., &c.

LONDON:

J. T. HAYES, LYALL PLACE, EATON SQUARE; AND
4, HENRIETTA STREET, COVENT GARDEN.

LONDON:

SWIFT AND CO., REGENT PRESS, KING STREET,

REGENT STREET, W.

CONTENTS.

CHAPTER I.—1206-1210.

CHAPTER II.—1210-1215.

CHAPTER III.—1216-1220.

CHAPTER XIII.—1228.

CHAPTER XIV.—1228.

CHAPTER XV.—1228.

CHAPTER XVI.—1228-1229.

CHAPTER XXI.—1231.

CHAPTER XXII.—

PREFACE.

———◆———

THE practical utility of religious biography, when the objects are wisely selected and fitly treated, is that it serves to show Christianity in action as a life, and not merely in theory as a speculation. No kind of literary composition has been more misused, from the narrowness, credulity, or partisanship of biographers. For they have by overloading their heroes with indiscriminate praise, or by heaping up gradual accretions of miracles over the simple record of the original facts—as in the later lives of S. Francis Xavier—or yet again by singling out for admiring comment exactly the least beautiful and saintlike episodes of the life, but most level to a formal and unspiritual mind, caused actual repulsion from the ideal they were fain to depict, and inspired readers in general with the profoundest distrust of their statements and conclusions.

And yet it is impossible to read any life of a human being who had a higher ambition than mere sensual enjoyment or worldly success, without coming on gleams of light which irradiate dark places in our thoughts, and help us to understand that hardest of all problems, ourselves. It is little matter what the era, the opinions, or the outward circumstances of the subject of a biography may be, so long as we have the facts of his life put as truthfully before us as may be, and Sakya-muni, the Indian prince; Epictetus, the Greek slave; Fodheil, the Arab robber; each and all can teach us lessons as true and wholesome in kind, though not in degree, as the hagiography of Christian Saints. But when we can thus sit at the feet of one who believed as we believe, yet with a more fervid and living faith, a closer sympathy and a readier imitation are likely to come of it than when we read of those who are parted from us by almost complete divergence in matters of the highest thought; and it is with the hope of kindling this sympathy and rousing this spirit of imitation that the writer of this series of Church Biographies has undertaken her task.

They are not unfitly ushered in by the story of one
in whose life the elements of sober fact and fanciful
legend are singularly blended, and whose experiences,
to cite the words of one who has made her the
central figure of a graceful and vigorous dramatic
poem :

" Tell us how of old our saintly mothers
Schooled themselves by vigil, fast, and prayer ;
Learnt to love as Jesus loved before them,
While they bore the Cross which poor men bear.

Tell us how our stout crusading fathers
Fought and died for God, and not for gold ;
Let their love, their faith, their boyish daring,
Distance-mellowed, gild the days of old."

R. F. L.

INTRODUCTION.

FOREMOST amongst those fruits which the Spirit of Religious revival is bringing forth in this our day, stands the longing to know more than we have hitherto known of the Saints of the Catholic Church. We dive into ancient Martyrologies, and our hearts kindle as we read of the glorious death of those holy ones of old, whose "blood was indeed the seed of the Church." Then we pass on from primitive to mediæval times, and in the records of the Middle Ages we find the details of sacrifices as great and as noble as those martyrdoms of will and of deed of the early Christians; we find strength as heroic as that strength before which fierce beasts of prey quailed and trembled.

It is the story of one of these mediæval Saints that we would tell now—one who was a king's daughter, a royal maiden, a holy widow.

It may be argued that in the life of S. Elizabeth of Hungary there is something that savours of unreality; indeed it has often been said that she forgot the duties of her high station, and made herself poor and humble, and took upon herself tasks which were not consistent with her royal dignity.

We will not stop here to refute these arguments. But there was One Who left His bright Home above, and His Father's Throne, and who lived as the poorest and most despised of the Sons of men; and she whose history we are going to tell sought by a life of poverty and self-abnegation to draw nearer to her Lord and Saviour. Let worldlings therefore judge her as they will, but let none presume to censure her.

The facts we have narrated here, are drawn from various sources, Catholic and Protestant; but many of the incidents we have recorded would never have been brought to light had not Charles Count de Montalembert sought for them amongst the old chronicles of " the dear Elizabeth's " country, and in his beautiful life of the Royal Saint, given them to the world. He who was a very Sir Galahad, in the purity of his stainless life, was indeed strangely well fitted to be the biographer of the gentle, modest lady, who was the ideal of his young manhood.

" May the perusal of this story " of S. Elizabeth " teach us to love the works in which the Saints delighted " (we are here quoting the words of the revered Dr. John Mason Neale, whose greatest earthly happiness was the contemplation of those holy ones who had given up all for Christ's sake) " for which Queens laid aside the royal attire, Abbesses the Pastoral Staff, Princesses the pomp and luxury of a Court, and all self."

S. ELIZABETH OF HUNGARY.

CHAPTER I.—1206-1210.

The Church in the Twelfth and Thirteenth Centuries — Andrew
II. of Hungary — Hermann, Landgrave of Thuringia — The
Prediction of Klingsohr the Hungarian Astrologer — The Birth
of the Princess Elizabeth — Her Early Piety — Duke Hermann's Embassy to the Court of Hungary — The little Princess
is carried to Thuringia — The Betrothal.

THE end of the twelfth century had closed darkly
enough upon the nations of Europe, and something of
the shadow of a cloud seemed to have fallen upon the
Church; the voice of the great S. Bernard had been
drowned amid the din and clamour of war, the Holy
City, for which the blood of the Crusaders had flown
in crimson streams, was still in the hands of the
infidels, the Crescent had triumphed over the Cross,
and fear fell upon men's minds, and hope died out of
many a brave heart.

The strife of nations continued during the thirteenth
century, but in the Church God raised up faithful
ones to do His work, to battle for Him against sin, the
world, and the devil. We hear of S. Louis of France,
of S. Ferdinand of Spain, of S. Francis d'Assisi, of

B

S. Dominic of Guzman, of S. Thomas Aquinas the
Angelic Doctor, and of many others whose names are
written in the Book of Life, and whose light shone
before men in this age of mediæval holiness. It was
at this time too that S. Elizabeth of Hungary lived,
and loved, and suffered and died, and has left to us the
bright example of her short life, that we, seeing her
good works, may glorify our Father Which is in
Heaven. Since the conversion of Hungary to the
Christian faith, her kings and princes had in turn been
numbered amongst the Saints of the Church of God;
and now in the dawn of the thirteenth century,
Andrew, the reigning monarch, well bore out the Greek
meaning of his name, which is rendered in that
language: *Manhood*, *Fortitude*, and *Valour*. This
wise and good king had married Gertrude, the daughter
of the Duke of Carinthia and Istria, and Lord of the
Tyrol, and one of her sisters was S. Hediwige of
Poland.

Queen Gertrude was a fitting wife for the noble king
of Hungary, a fitting mother for the Saint whom she
was destined to bring into the world. An old historian has quaintly described her character: "She
being admired for her rare beauty and princely
parentage was yet more amiable to the world for her
sage prudence, and fair demeanours; for which she
was more esteemed, than for the lilies and roses of her
cheeks, and greater lustre of her family."

Amongst the most powerful of the German princes contemporary with Andrew of Hungary, was Hermann, Landgrave of Thuringia and Hesse, and Count Palatine of Saxony. Hermann was a noble Christian knight and warrior, the special favourite of the Pope Innocent III., the near relative of Odoacer of Bohemia, and of Federick Barbarossa. His dominions extended from the Lahn to the Elbe, his powerful influence made itself felt throughout the whole empire. It was said of him that he could make kings at his pleasure, and raise or crush kingdoms by one single word. He was famous for his power, but a yet more enviable distinction was his ; he was renowned in all the Courts of Europe for his many virtues, and his sincere piety ; whilst his noble, generous, chivalrous spirit won for him the name of " the Flower of Thuringia." He had spent his youth in Paris, and from thence he carried into his own country a love of learning and of poetry, which he cultivated amongst his people for the rest of his life.

The noblest of the poets of Germany were often assembled at his Court ; and in the year 1206 it chanced that ten of these learned men were there, and none could determine the merits of the rival minstrels or assign to any one amongst the number the palm of victory. All the highest nobles of the land had come together to hear the songs of the poets, and to decide who amongst them all, was entitled to take precedence amongst his fellows; but when they had listened to the grand recitals of war, and chivalry, and religion, they knew not to whom to give the poet's crown.

Now, at the Court of the King of Hungary there lived one Maître Klingsohr, an astrologer, whose fame for wisdom and learning had reached Thuringia, and it was agreed that he should be asked to settle the point at issue.

A messenger was sent to entreat him to come to the Landgrave's court, and in due time Klingsohr arrived at Eisenach, where Hermann and the nobles were assembled. Crowds soon flocked around the learned man, eager and anxious to hear him tell some of those marvellous things, for which he was so famed. For a time he was silent; then he looked into the anxious, expectant faces which were turned to him, and he said: "You want me to tell you something new. I will do so, and it is joyful news that you will hear from me this evening. I see a fair and beautiful star rising in Hungary, shining from thence to Marburg, and from Marburg over the whole earth. Know that this very night there is born to my lord the King of Hungary, a daughter, who shall be named Elizabeth, and who shall be given in marriage to a prince of this country; she shall be a great Saint, and her holiness shall be the joy and consolation of Christendom."

There was great joy amongst the people of Thuringia when they heard these wonderful words of the astrologer; they were duly repeated to the Landgrave, and he sent for Klingsohr to his palace, and loaded him with honours, and after he had fulfilled the purpose for which he came, and decided the claims of the rival poets, he returned to his own country of Hungary. In the meantime what he had predicted had come to pass, a little daughter had been born to good Queen Gertrude, and the child had been carried to church with great pomp, and baptized by the name of Elizabeth.

Very early in life the little one began to show signs of that saintliness for which she was afterwards distinguished. The sacred words of religion were amongst the first words her baby lips learned to frame; the holy names of the Infant Saviour, and of His Virgin Mother, were lisped by her with touching reverence. Very eagerly she listened to her gentle mother's first simple lessons in the great truths of the Christian faith. Anxiously, as other children ask to be told some amusing story, would she beg to be told of all the love of the Holy Child Jesus.

At the sight of some poor beggar, tears of compassion would start to the child-like, trusting eyes, and she would only be comforted by being allowed to bestow her alms upon " God's own poor."

It has been rightly said of her that "her first deed was an alms, her first word a prayer;" in every action of the baby life there seemed to shine forth a promise of that future holiness which has caused her name to be enrolled amongst the Saints of the Catholic Church.

It seemed too that a special blessing came to the country of Elizabeth with the first germ of the pure young life into which God had breathed the spirit of His own Divine Love. There had been foreign wars and home troubles devastating Hungary during the earlier parts of the reign of Andrew II.; these all ceased after the birth of the young Princess, and the brave Hungarians looked with special veneration upon the child who already had wrought such good in the land they loved so well.

There were other eyes too, turned upon the little Elizabeth with longing anxious gaze. Duke Hermann had of course taken care to enquire whether Klingsohr's prediction had been fulfilled; and when he was told that a daughter had been born to the King of Hungary, and when he heard, moreover, of the early proofs of piety which the little one had already displayed, and the blessings she had brought down upon her own land, he became most anxious that the remainder of the astrologer's prophecy should be accomplished, and that the little Hungarian Princess should be the bride of his young son Louis.

He sent an embassy consisting of noble lords and ladies, into Hungary, to ask the king to give his little daughter to the heir of Thuringia, and he begged that Elizabeth might be sent back with his messengers to the country of her future husband.

The deputation arrived at Presburg, and were received with every mark of esteem and honour; they laid their cause before the king and queen, they told of all the child-like goodness and amiability of the little Louis.

Andrew listened to all they had to say, but the heart which had never quailed in moments of deepest danger, trembled and shrank at the thought of parting from his darling only daughter, who had brought such peace to his country and his house. His wife, however, took the side of the Thuringians, and urged all the wisdom and advantage of such an alliance; the king yielded to her influence, and his voice trembled as he spoke those words which were to send his little helpless child " far away from her own people and her father's house."

All was settled; a great feast was held, which lasted for three days, and when the music and song and dancing had ceased, Elizabeth, a loving, gentle little maiden of scarce four years old, was clad in a silken robe and laid in a silver cradle, and presented to the Thuringians, to be carried by them to the country of her adoption.

The king gave her into the especial charge of Gaultier Lord of Varilla, saying: "I entrust my greatest earthly blessing to your knightly honour;" to which Varilla replied: " I receive her willingly into my keeping, and will be faithful to her for ever;" a promise which in the dark and troubled days that were to come, was right loyally kept by the Thuringian noble.

The last loving kisses had been pressed upon the baby cheek by her fond parents, .the last words of whispered blessing spoken, and then the little princess journeyed with the ambassadors, and with the thirteen Hungarian maidens, whom her father had given her to be her companions and attendants, towards her new far away home.

The Landgrave, and his wife the Duchess Sophia, received their future daughter with every mark of love. Hermann took the child into his arms, and thanked God for having given her to his son, and then he went forward to his castle of Wartburg to prepare for the princess's reception, whilst the duchess spent the whole night watching by her side.

The next day in the presence of the nobles and burghers of Eisenach the little girl of four years old, and the noble boy over whose head only eleven summers had passed, were solemnly betrothed, and then there were great rejoicings and feastings through-out all the land, and Elizabeth never again left him whom she learned to love so tenderly, and whom in the years to come she mourned so truly.

In accordance with the custom of the times the children called each other "brother" and "sister," and when the childish love deepened into more passionate devotion, they still retained the pure endearing names, mingling them at last with the sacred titles of " husband " and " wife ;" thus calming and sanctifying the later tie by the sweet memories of those early, innocent years, upon which they ever loved to dwell.

Never again did " the dear Elizabeth," as the Germans still love to call her, leave the country of her adoption, except when once in the years that were to come she paid a short visit to her father's court and her childhood's home.

CHAPTER II.—1210-1215.

The childish years of Elizabeth — The death of her mother, the
Good Queen Gertrude — How, day by day, the love for all
holy things grew in the young Princess's heart — S. John
the Evangelist becomes Elizabeth's patron Saint — Her
earnest self-denial, and longing to give up all for the sake
of Christ.

MONTHS passed on, and in the far away land of
Thuringia the little Elizabeth was the same gentle,
pious child who had listened so eagerly in her own
home in Hungary to the loving lessons which fell
from the lips of good Queen Gertrude.

She had, too, before her childish eyes two bright
examples of Christian life ; the one in her father-in-law,
the noble and God-fearing Duke Hermann ; the other
in her maternal aunt Hediwige, Duchess of Poland,
who was a most holy woman, and was canonized after
her death, because of the fervent piety and strict
austerity she had practised in that high station in
which God had placed her.   For her the young
Hungarian princess conceived a strange attachment ;. to
imitate her, and be like her, became the ruling passion
of Elizabeth's life.   Very soon trouble came to the
child, the greatest that can come into the life of God's

children. The good Queen Gertrude died two years after Elizabeth had left her home, and the circumstances attending her death were fraught with such bitter sorrow to all who loved her, that they made a more than usually vivid impression upon the child's mind, and from that sad day she was more thoughtful and earnest than she had been before.

Gertrude had died for the sake of her husband. A conspiracy was formed against the king, and to give him time to fly, she stood all calm and brave before his enemies, and their cruel, dastardly blows fell upon her head.

No marvel that the story of the manner of her mother's death left a deep impress upon the heart of the gentle child; no marvel that she determined from henceforth to live more nearly to God; to become more like the Holy Jesus, Who is the Pattern of all Christian children. Her father-in-law had chosen seven noble Thuringian maidens to be her companions, amongst them was his own daughter Agnes. Another of them was named Guta; she remained faithful to the Saint amid all the vicissitudes of her short and troubled life, and to her simple and touching narrative we owe the knowledge of the details of the young princess' early years. Very often when her companions were amusing themselves with their toys and their little games, Elizabeth would steal into the chapel, and although she could not read, she would open a large Psalter, and kneel at the Altar steps, her tiny hands clasped, her pure, innocent·eyes raised trustfully to heaven.

Thus, in her childish way, she would pray and meditate; and surely her Angel Guardian carried the unspoken words to the Golden Gate, and laid them at the Feet of Him she so faithfully strove to serve.

At other times she would propose to the other children that they should all run races, and see who first should reach the chapel; and if by chance the door was locked, she would kiss the locks and walls which shut her out from the Holy Presence into which she so longed to enter.

Her every action seemed ruled by the spirit of child-like love and obedience which were ever her especial characteristics, which seemed somehow to be a part of the little Elizabeth's nature. To serve God was the one thought of her life, and to pray to Him as often as she wished, made her occasionally resort to an innocent *ruse*, to which in after-life she sometimes alluded. "Let us lie down on the grass," she would say to her little companions, "and see which of us is the tallest." The children of course eagerly acceded to the proposal, and the little princess stretched herself in turn by the side of each of the little girls, and took the opportunity of worshipping God, and repeating a *Pater* and an *Ave*.

Often the little party would wander to the church-yard, and then Elizabeth would speak in her grave, childish way of the uncertainty of all earthly things. " Remember that we shall all one day become dust. All those who are lying here once lived as we live, and are now dead just as we too must die ; it is for this reason that we must love God. Let us kneel down and say, ' Oh, Lord, by Thy cruel death, and for the sake of Thy Blessed Mother, deliver these souls from their trouble ; Oh, Lord, save us by Thy Five most Sacred Wounds.' "

To speak to the child of high and holy things was at once to find the way to her heart. She had learned a number of prayers, which she set herself to say each day, and if, when night came, any of them were by some unavoidable accident left unsaid, she lay awake, even as the holy David of old, praying, and remembering God in her bed. Her charity in those early years was unbounded, almost lavish. All that was given her she sought to bestow upon the poor ; and often the little lady was to be found in the kitchen, to the great annoyance of the servants, picking up scraps, which she took to the Castle gates to feed the beggars who waited for her there. It was the custom of those times to draw a patron saint out of the number of the twelve Apostles, and Elizabeth, who had already placed herself under the especial protection of the Blessed Virgin, hoped and prayed that to her lot might fall the Disciple of Love, the holy Evangelist S. John.

The day came upon which the trial was to be made ;
the names of the twelve Apostles were written upon
twelve wax tapers, which were mixed together, and
placed upon the altar, whilst each child in turn drew
one hap-hazard. The taper which bore the name of S.
John became the property of Elizabeth, and she was
so rejoiced at this answer to her simple prayers, that
she asked that she might be allowed to try again.
Three times the ceremony was repeated, three times
did the little girl draw the taper upon which the name
of S. John was inscribed, and then she knew indeed
that he who, out of the depth of his love to God, had
learned to love his fellow-men, was to be her patron
and blessed example for all her life.

To be more worthy of this sacred patronage, to be
more loving and gentle and charitable to all around
her, was now the aim of Elizabeth's life. Child
though she was, she began to practise voluntary
humiliation and austerity. On Sundays and fête
days, when her companions delighted to dress themselves in their best clothes, and to adorn their small
persons with laces and jewels, she, the highest born
and the noblest amongst them all, would appear
simply attired, her dress devoid of all ornament, nothing
but a Crucifix suspended round her fair neck. There
were few opportunities in her luxurious life for the
practice of rigorous austerities ; and so it was in small
things that she sought to bend and break her somewhat

impetuous will, and that she laid the seeds of that total self-abnegation and submission to God in all things, which in after life caused great men, ay, and great Saints too, to look on and wonder.

When in the midst of her childish games she grew eager and excited, and longed to go on, she would suddenly stop "for the love of God." And in the giddy dance, as she whirled joyously round, the same thoughts came to her mind: to stop, to give up the pleasure, would be to forego something for Jesus' sake; and many and many a time she walked quietly away to sit by herself and muse upon the love of God. And yet, amid all this, she was ever bright and joyous, she seemed to carry sunshine with her wherever she went; even when in after years sorrow came to her, and that earthly love upon which she had so leaned was crushed out of her heart, and she endured untold agony of soul and spirit, the sweet chastened gaiety of her early years was still to be seen, it could not be crushed out by anguish or bereavement, for it was God's own gift of peace to His faithful servant.

The troubles that came to her were from without, sent to her straight from heaven. Other saints have endured temptations, have had to battle against what seemed almost insurmountable obstacles in their spiritual life and progress. No such storms ever darkened the star which had shone upon S. Elizabeth's cradle, and which shone with brighter and yet brighter radiance until it rested upon her grave. Hard indeed was her onward way, beset with many a sorrow, but she thanked God that she was counted worthy to walk in the Foot-prints of her Lord, and her stedfast eyes were ever fixed upon her own true country, and by faith she beheld the glory that should some day be revealed to her.

The thorns of adversity became as bright, sweet roses—her own especial flower—in her path; truly in her life was verified the truth of that lovely proverb of another land: " When thou fearest, then GOD is nearest."

CHAPTER III.—1216-1220.

The death of the young Princess' father-in-law, the Landgrave
Hermann — Troubles come into the child's life — Her gentleness and amiability — Her sorrow when tempted to give way
to impatience — Elizabeth before the Crucifix in the Church
of Eisenach — Her Troubles increase — Young Louis of Thuringia — The dawning of brighter days — The Wedding in the
Castle of Wartburg.

ELIZABETH was only nine years old when, in the year
1216, the second great sorrow came upon her. The
brave and good Landgrave Hermann died; and the
child whom he had loved so tenderly was left to the
care of those who were impatient with her because
her wish to serve God came before all else, and who
were determined upon making her give up those pious
practices which had made her all the more dear and
precious to the kind friend who had been taken from
her.

Young Louis, her affianced husband, loved his "little
sister" deeply and truly; but he was still a mere boy,
and the guardianship of the young Hungarian princess
was entrusted to his mother the Duchess Sophia, who
took no pains to conceal the displeasure she felt at
witnessing the child's devotion to her religious
duties.

C

The Princess Agnes, Louis' sister, a maiden of surpassing beauty, was for ever reproaching Elizabeth for her quiet, unassuming, gentle ways, and told her in very plain language that she was fit only to be a housemaid, and that she had better not aspire to be her brother's wife. The companions of the two young princesses were only too ready to follow the lead of the lovely Agnes, and by degrees a strong party was formed against the innocent Elizabeth; she was laughed at, ridiculed, insulted, and she bore all patiently—only she withdrew herself more and more from the society of those who so misjudged her; and she sought out the poor in the neighbourhood of Eisenach, and whilst she gave her alms to the mothers, she loved to gather the little ragged children around her, and speak to them in simple words of God and of heaven.

In her heart there was no angry feeling against her persecutors; her unhappiness only seemed to draw her more closely to her Saviour; she sought to love those who had created a new link between her and her Lord. But her loving gentleness failed to win their hearts; still the cruel jests and mocking taunts sounded in her ears, and the hot blood would sometimes mount to the fair young cheek, and the light of just indignation flash in the dark eye.

The indignation was but momentary, the sorrow for having given way to it lasted many a long hour; for Elizabeth fixed her mind on her loving and forgiving Saviour, and she bowed her head in very shame, and acknowledged that often and often she had offended against Him, Who loved her so well that He died for her.

One day—it was the Feast of the Assumption of the Blessed Virgin—the princesses and their young companions accompanied the Duchess Sophia to Eisenach, in order to be present at Mass.

Elizabeth and Agnes, clad in their richest attire in obedience to the Duchess' orders, and with golden crowns upon their heads, knelt in the beautiful church before a large crucifix.

Tearfully and reverently Elizabeth gazed upon the life-like Figure of her bleeding, dying Saviour; and taking off her golden crown, she prostrated herself upon the ground, whilst her black hair, escaping from its confinement, fell in loose luxuriance around her slender person.

The Duchess was very angry when she saw what the young girl had done. "What is the matter with you?" she said brusquely. "What new absurdity are you going to be guilty of; what new folly are you going to commit, so that all the world may laugh at you, and turn you into ridicule? Young ladies ought to hold themselves upright, and not throw themselves upon the ground like mad women, or old nuns who bend about like broken reeds. Can you not behave as we do, instead of as an ill-bred child? Is your crown too heavy for you to bear, that you lie there bent double like a peasant ?"

Very humbly the young princess rose and stood before the Duchess. "Dear lady," she said, "be not angry with me. See there before my eyes my God and my King, that loving, merciful Jesus, Who is crowned with sharp thorns. How then can I, His vile creature, kneel before Him crowned with precious stones, and gold, and pearls ! My crown surely would be but a mockery of His." And then the poor child cried bitterly, not on account of the sharp and cruel words which the Duchess had spoken to her, but at the thought of those many woes which her Saviour had borne for her sake. Once more she knelt before the holy symbol of shame and of triumph ; and unmindful of the whispered, mocking words of those around her, she poured out all the love of her young heart to Him, the Crucified.

Day by day things grew worse, Elizabeth's enemies were the great and powerful nobles of the Court, who all tried to turn the young Landgrave against his affianced bride, and to persuade him to send her back to her own country. The Duchess and the Princess Agnes joined their entreaties to those of the courtiers, and the former sought to induce her future daughter-in-law to take the veil.

But the child loved Louis truly ; from her earliest infancy she had been taught to look upon herself as his affianced bride; she could not give him up now, that "dear brother," who had ever been so good and kind to her. She took her trouble to God, she laid it at the foot of the Cross, and when she took up the burden again it was light and easy, for she was bearing it for Jesus' sake, and to His tender keeping she committed herself in these words:

"O Sovereign Spouse of my heart, suffer me not to desire that which Thou dost not desire, let all things else be ungrateful and bitter to me, and Thou only sweet. That Thy Will be mine, and this my desire withal, that as in Heaven Thy Will is ever done, so may it be done likewise here on earth, and most particularly by me. And since love requires an union, and a most entire resignation of all things into the hands of the beloved, I give myself to Thee without reserving aught to myself, I renounce all the riches and pomps of this world, and if I had many worlds, I would leave them all for Thee and become poor, as Thou wast poor for me. O, Spouse of my heart, so great is the love I bear Thee, and poverty for Thy sake, that if it were possible I would leave to be what I am, to be transformed into Thee. My enemies seek to overthrow and to entrap me, and with their guiles to draw me from Thy service. O let them not prevail upon my weakness, but be Thou a rampart to me against the assaults and batteries they lay against me, to take me from my settled purpose of following

Thee, as nearly as my state and condition will permit. I trust Thou wilt perfect what Thou hast begun, and I shall remain victorious over all my adversaries: This I beseech Thee, for Thy beloved servant's sake S. John, my patron, for the love of Thy dearest Mother, and above all for Thy Most Precious Blood, wherein I put my chiefest trust."

He in Whom she trusted was ever with her; a brighter day was dawning upon the girl's life; for a time, for a few brief years it was to be given her to taste the full happiness of an almost perfect earthly affection.

There was one who never laughed at her, who loved her better as day by day he witnessed her saint-like patience, her gentle submission beneath the taunts and railings of her enemies; and this one was the young Landgrave, her affianced husband. His whole soul was moved with pity for her; the more he saw the hatred of others showered upon her innocent head, the more he determined that it should be his task to chase away the dark clouds of sorrow, and to brighten the young life into which so much suffering had already come.

What others condemned was his greatest joy; the sweet youthful modesty, the simple attire, the retiring manners of the Princess Elizabeth, all drew her more closely into the brave, chivalrous young heart, which sought only to imitate one so good and so pious. He dared not openly show all his love for the gentle girl; he was afraid that to do so would only draw upon her fresh indignities from his mother and sister; it was only when she sat alone, bowed down by the cruel treatment she received, that he sought her out, and poured into her ears the tale of his love, and bade her wait but a little while and all would be well.

Often Louis had to leave the Castle of Wartburg to attend to the affairs of his dominions, and he never came back from these journeys without bringing Elizabeth some little token of his love ; something which showed her that she had been in his thoughts during those long, weary days of his absence from her side. Once only he returned and brought no present with him; and Elizabeth, who had been more than usually tormented by her enemies, resented the seeming neglect, whilst the courtiers rejoiced at it, and hailed it as a sign that Louis was cooling in his love towards the young Hungarian princess. The girl heard their whispered words; and meeting Gaultier, Lord of Varilla, into whose keeping her father had given her, and who had ever been her trusty friend and champion, she confided to him the sorrow that weighed so deeply upon her heart.

Gaultier promised to speak on the subject to his young master.

Two or three days afterwards he kept his word. He went out hunting with Louis; and when they were resting in a wood, above which towered Inselberg, the highest of the Thuringian mountains, Gaultier thus addressed the Landgrave :

"My lord, will you answer me a question I am about to ask you ?"

"Undoubtedly," answered Louis; "speak as you will, I will answer anything you choose to ask me."

"Then will you tell me," continued Gaultier, "what you purpose doing with the Lady Elizabeth, whom I brought to you from Hungary? Will you take her for your wife, or will you break your plighted word, and send her back to her father ?"

Then Louis rose hastily and indignantly, and stretched out his hand towards the lofty mountain of Inselberg.

"Do you see that mountain," he said; "know then that if it were of purest gold from its base to its summit, and if I were told that it should all be mine on condition that I sent away my Elizabeth, I would not do it. Let others say and think what they will, that is naught to me; I love her better than all else on earth, and I am determined that she shall be mine. Her virtue and her piety are dearer to me than all the world."

"My lord," said Gaultier, "have I your permission to repeat your words to the princess."

"Tell her all," answered Louis eagerly; "tell her too that I will never listen to those who try to set me against her, and give her this as a new pledge of my faith ;" and the Landgrave put into the courtier's hands a little double-cased mirror, wherein was a picture of our crucified Lord.

With all speed the trusty knight sought the young princess, and told her all that Louis had said, and gave her the pledge of his love and faith.

Joyfully indeed did she receive it ; how could she doubt him any more, when it seemed as though his affection for her was based upon *His* love, Who loves us first and best.

In 1218, the young Landgrave, having entered upon his nineteenth year, received the sword of knighthood in the church of S. George at Eisenach, from the hands of the Bishop of Nuremburg. No foreign prince was there, for Louis had declared that he would only hold his knighthood from God and from his vassals. The following year he engaged in his first campaign, a war against the rapacious Archbishop of Mayence, whom he obliged to sue for peace. On his return to Thuringia he boldly announced his intention of no longer delaying his marriage, and he ordered all those who had sought to injure Elizabeth, by word or deed, to be silent from henceforth. His firmness took all by surprise, none dared disobey him, or seek to turn him from his fixed purpose ; and in 1220 the wedding took place with great pomp in the chapel of the Castle of Wartburg, and the young bridegroom received his bride from the hands of the faithful Gaultier, Lord of Varilla, who nine years before had sworn to the King of Hungary that he would watch over and protect his child.

He to whom he resigned his trust was indeed well worthy of the treasure God had given him. With the exception of his noble namesake S. Louis of France, the annals of the thirteenth century tell of no prince who united in his person, even at the early age of twenty years, all the virtues of a Christian knight and prince, as did Louis of Thuringia "the good Land-grave." Tall, athletic, well made, the beauty of his person was but a mirror of the rare beauty of his mind; the purity of his soul shone forth in the serene and sweet expression of his face. All the historians of the age in which he lived agree in saying that there was a striking resemblance in him to that portrait which tradition has handed down to us as His, Who for our sakes became Incarnate. The sweetness of Louis' smile was irresistible, his bearing was noble and courteous, his voice was low and soft, and yet most manly; to see him was to love him, and to trust in him above all other men. Truly, he was a noble, chivalrous knight, "sans peur et sans reproche," he was fearless almost to recklessness; and yet he was modest and chaste as any girl, an impure word would cause him to blush; he was silent and reserved in his speech, lest he should in any way commit a sin of the tongue. To women he was strangely courteous, to little children ever most tender and pitiful, to the poor always gentle and affable. Unscathed he had passed through all the temptations of youth. Left to himself when he was a boy of sixteen, master of one of the richest kingdoms in Germany, surrounded by all that wealth and luxury could give him, he turned a deaf ear to the insidious flatteries of his courtiers, and he never wavered from the path in which he had sworn before God that he would walk, never suffered one shadow to tarnish the brightness of that device which as a boy he had chosen and caused to be emblazoned on his shield. " Piety, chastity, justice ;" in fact, the latter virtue seems to have been his only passion, and it was well that it was so ; for the love of justice caused him to punish those who violated the laws, whilst his natural kindness might have allowed the offender to escape.

And to this model of all knightly perfection and Christian chivalry, the Lord of Varilla consigned the keeping of the child (even now she was but thirteen years old) he had brought all those years ago from her distant home. Brightly indeed was the sun shining upon those two young lives. Loving each other with a pure and holy love in Christ their Lord, they stand out as bright examples of that mystical union between Christ and His Church, of which marriage is a symbol and a type. They sought to help each other on, in

the path of perfection; they knew that to love God
first, and before all, was to sanctify, and purify their
love for each other, and so they started together on
life's journey, not seeking to avoid the sorrows and
troubles of the world, but learning to meet them,
striving amid all their happiness to bear Him ever
in their hearts, under Whose banner they had promised to serve. And they knew that that banner was
the banner of the Cross; and the tale that the Cross
tells us is one of the direst sufferings that was ever
endured by man; but God be thanked, that suffering
leads to joy unspeakable, which eye has never seen, of
which ear has never heard.

CHAPTER IV.—1220-1221.

The first years of Elizabeth's married life — Her growing
 devotion — Her austerity of life — The mutual love of the
 young couple — Elizabeth's acts of charity to the poor and the
 sick — Her special care for lepers — Sundry anecdotes setting
 forth her childish zeal and faith.

JUST as there have been great Saints to whom temptations have come from within, which it seemed almost
impossible to overcome, so there have been others who
have felt that if they would give their whole hearts
and lives to God, they must tear away all earthly
affection, wrench from the very fibres of their being
all that to them was nearest and dearest. But with
" the dear Elizabeth " it was not so, the love that
she bestowed upon all around her, was but a reflection
of the holier, higher love which was given with all the
intensity of her nature to Him Who died for her.
Deep and tender though the affection was which she
entertained for her young husband, it never interfered
with one single act of devotion, never cut short one
single prayer. She obeyed him with gentle submission as it beseems a wife to do ; she sought to please
him in all things, to ward off from him every care,
every annoyance, to make his home so bright and

happy that when his duties called him away, his one wish was to get back to his young and loving wife.

Truly the life that in those few short years had known so much of sorrow and of bitterness, was now as one long summer's day in its gladness and its joy; and yet Elizabeth never for an instant ceased to meditate upon that most sacred life of suffering which had brought into the world such infinite, inestimable joy. Night after night when her husband slept, she would rise from her soft couch and kneel upon the floor, and think of that cold winter's night when, more than twelve hundred years before, the Child Jesus was born in the lonely Manger at Bethlehem; the chill wind blowing around Him, the pitiless blast telling in wailing tones, of the sorrows that yet must come to the God Man.

Louis would sometimes seek to moderate her zeal, and bid her care for her health as a precious gift given her from heaven to be used to the greater glory of God, but in his heart he loved his Elizabeth all the better for her pious practices, and in all her works of charity and deeds of love he was ever a most willing helper.

Long and rigidly she fasted, so that by such discipline her flesh might be subdued, and she might walk more humbly before God. Always beneath her silken robe she wore a shirt of hair; every Friday of the year, and every day during the holy season of Lent, she caused her attendants to strike her with cords, in memory of Him Whose sacred flesh was torn and scourged, and lacerated, for our sakes. And when the cruel, self-imposed discipline, had been performed, she would appear, all bright and smiling, as though she had endured no such pain as that which must have been hers. She entered into all the amusements and gaieties befitting her rank and station, it was no part of her religion to make herself disagreeable and morose to others. She was wont to say of those who affected any undue solemnity of manner, "they seem as if they wished to frighten the good God; why do they not serve Him cheerfully, and with a good will?" Her Confessor at this time was Father Conrad, of Marburg, to whom she had taken, with her husband's permission, a vow of obedience, so long as such obedience did not interfere with her wifely duties.

Certain taxes had been laid by the Landgrave's ministers upon sundry articles of necessary food, which were daily to be found upon the tables of the Castle of Wartburg; Father Conrad, who had set himself against these acts of oppression, forbade the Duchess to taste of the viands, which were procured, he said, by robbing the poor. She obeyed most willingly, although such submission often obliged her to turn away fasting from the rich banquets where she presided at her husband's side; a crust of dry bread was many a time her only food, and yet she never mur-

mured at her Confessor's decree; only when on certain occasions she was told that there was no forbidden meat upon the table, she would clap her hands with child-like joyousness, and say, "We shall be well off to-day; we may eat and drink without fear of doing wrong."

She was never quite happy when Louis was away from her; often she would accompany him on his distant journeys, and she would undergo any amount of fatigue, bear the burning heat of summer and the piercing cold of winter, if only she might be at her "dear brother's" side—if only she might hear the sound of his loved voice. Sometimes, indeed, the young Landgrave had to leave his own dominions, and go into other countries where he could not take his lovely young wife; but these short absences only served to show both how necessary each was to the other's happiness; of all the fair and beautiful ladies he saw in the Courts of other sovereigns, there was not one who in Louis' eyes would bear comparison with his own Elizabeth. She, in her turn, when he was obliged to leave her, laid aside the rich and costly garments which she wore but to please him, and put on the sober dress of a widow, spending the time he was away from her in yet longer fasts and more devout prayers.

One day, the old chroniclers tell us, the husband was absent from his fair young wife, and she sat alone at

her solitary meal of bread and water. The Landgrave returned unexpectedly, and laughingly stooped to
drink out of her cup. It contained, to his surprise, not
water, but wine more delicious than any he had ever
yet tasted, and he asked the steward of his household
from whence it came? The man replied, in utter
astonishment, that his lady never drank anything but
pure water. Louis made no further comment, but he
knew that He Who had turned the water into wine
at the marriage feast of Cana of Galilee, had
blessed the cup of cold water which Elizabeth had
poured out for herself, that she might bestow the more
costly drink upon God's poor. There were those in
her husband's Court who looked upon that earnest,
watchful life of self-denial, and publicly reproached
Elizabeth for it, even blaming Louis for allowing such
extravagances. But neither of the young people cared
much for the world's praise or the world's blame ; they
had set before their minds but one duty, that of
pleasing God in all things, and the jests and taunts
of ungodly men fell all unheeded on their ears.

More stories are told us of Elizabeth's gentle charity
than we can find room for in this short chronicle of
her simple, blameless life, but a few of them must be
given here just as they have been handed down to us by
the chroniclers of the times in which she lived, who
have told us in quaint poetical language of her many
noble deeds, and of the miracles which showed how

D

acceptable her prayers and her alms-deeds were in the sight of God.

Already we have seen how when she was but a little girl she had refused to wear a golden crown, as she knelt before the figure of her thorn-crowned Saviour; and as years went on that feeling of intense humility deepened in her mind, and she resolved always to dress as simply as she possibly could, only to attire herself in the silken robes of state when her husband bade her thus appear before his people. It chanced that one day she went into the town of Eisenach richly dressed, and crowned with her golden crown. As usual crowds followed her, asking the charity which they knew was never refused. Elizabeth had no money with her, but she took off all her ornaments and placed them in the eagerly extended hands of the beggars. She had given away all she had, and still one poor man was left upon whom no jewels had been bestowed. The young Duchess knew not what to give him, and yet she could not send him away starving, and not in some way help him. She quickly took off one of her gloves, which was richly embroidered and ornamented with precious stones, and handed it to the beggar in her own gracious manner. A brave young knight, who had witnessed the scene, followed the poor man, and gave him a sum of money in exchange for the glove, which he fastened upon his helmet, as a badge of Divine protection. From that moment he was successful in all he undertook, he triumphed over all his enemies, and was never again vanquished by them. In after years he fought in the Crusades, and his name ranked amongst the bravest of all Christian knights. He returned to his native land laden with honours, and he always said that he attributed all his success to that precious glove which once belonged to " the dear Elizabeth." The young duchess won for herself the proud sweet name of " Patroness of the Poor." It was not because of her rich and costly gifts that this title was assigned to her, it was because she went day by day from her luxurious palace to the dwellings of the sick and of the suffering, and nursed and tended her brothers and sisters in Christ, speaking to them in gentle words, bidding them think of Him Who endured such extremities of agony for their sakes upon the Cross. In many a wretched home her bright presence was to be found carrying a ray of sunshine where all had been so dark before. No distance, no difficulty was ever allowed to be an obstacle in her way, if there was any good to be done, any sorrow to be soothed and comforted. Mothers placed their little new-born babes in her arms, and the gentle lady would hold them at the baptismal font, and promise to care for them so long as she lived. Death had no terror for her. Often with her own hands, tenderly and reverently as though they had been her own loved ones, she washed and laid out the corpses of the poorest of her subjects; often she would carry to the homes of the poor the food she knew they so sorely needed, and thus laden she would descend the steep mountain path which surrounded the Castle of Wartburg. One day she was thus occupied, when she came face to face with her husband, who was returning from a hunting party. Astonished at seeing her bending beneath the heavy burden she was carrying, he said, "Why, what have you here?" and at the same time drew aside her cloak, in order to satisfy his curiosity. Not caring that her good deeds should thus he made know to the courtiers who accompanied Louis, Elizabeth drew her mantle more closely round her, and sought to hide the food with which she was laden. It was too late; but she need not have feared, for naught was to be seen beneath her cloak but the most lovely red and white roses which it was possible to behold, — and this in the depth of winter, when the snow lay thick upon the ground. Seeing how troubled and agitated his wife was, Louis sought to caress her, but as he did so he drew back, for above her head he saw in the heavens a bright shining light, in the form of a Cross. Again he knew that this was a sign from God of His especial love for His saint. He did not speak to her of it, he bade her go on her errand of mercy, only he carried away one of the roses with him, and kept it near his heart all the rest of his life. And he ordered a pillar to be built at the place where he had met Elizabeth, and to be surmounted by a crucifix, in memory of that Holy Sign which he had seen shining above his wife's head.

To those who were afflicted with that most painful of all diseases, leprosy, the Duchess of Thuringia showed an especial compassion. It was a part of Mediæval Catholicity to treat those who were thus afflicted with something approaching to veneration; as men who bore in their own person all that weight of human woe which Jesus Christ had come to relieve, and whom it was the duty of all His faithful children to tend with more than common care. Dead to the world, living their lonely life either in a hospital or in some way-side hut, before the door of which was placed a wooden cross upon which hung an alms-box, to which Christian men and women dropped their offerings as they passed along the road, these poor lepers were only allowed at the joyful Easter feast to enter the towns and villages, and to rejoice for eight short days in the gladness of Christendom. Then they went back again to their desolate existence, the love and the prayers of the faithful following them into their solitude. To these poor wretches, separated from the world, marked by the Hand of God, Elizabeth was determined to minister with her own hand. She had no fear of contagion; she sought them out, sat by them, bade them be patient and trust in God, and assured them that such suffering as theirs, borne for Christ's sake, must win for them a sure reward hereafter. On Maundy Thursday she assembled around her twelve poor lepers, washed their hands and their feet, and knelt before them, and kissed their loathsome sores. Day after day her proud mother-in-law, the Duchess Sophia, saw all Elizabeth's gentleness, and goodness, and humility, and yet she was not won over by it; she persecuted her when she could, just as she had done in her childish days; and whenever her son was absent from the castle she took the opportunity of laughing at the saint, and turning her into ridicule in every possible way.

It happened on one occasion the Duke was away, and the young Duchess, seeing a poor leper, in whom she took a deep interest, deserted by all who knew him, and dying for want of care, took him to the castle, washed him, dressed his wounds, and then laid him in her own luxurious bed. While she was thus engaged Louis suddenly returned to Wartburg; his mother met him with a smile of envious triumph, saying, "Come with me, sweet son, and I will show you what your Elizabeth is doing now, what new folly she is guilty of." "What do you mean?" asked the astonished Duke. "Come with me," answered the proud lady, "and you will see who it is that she loves better than she loves you;" then she laid her hand upon his arm, and drew him to his own room, and made him stand by the side of his own bed. "See, sweet son, your wife places lepers in your bed, and I have no power to prevent it: she wishes to give you the leprosy; you can see this yourself."

Somewhat irritated at his mother's words, the Duke impatiently drew back the coverlid, but God opened his eyes, and instead of the poor diseased, leprous form, he saw the sacred figure of Jesus upon the Cross, stretched upon his bed. The Duchess Sophia saw it also, and both stood there silent and stupefied, and unable to utter a word. At last Louis gave way to bitter tears, and rushed from the room. His wife followed him, to try and turn away what she imagined to be his anger against the poor leper. "Elizabeth," he said, drawing her lovingly towards him, "my dear good sister, I beseech you often to give my bed to such guests as this: let no one hinder you in your good works."

Soon afterwards Elizabeth obtained her husband's permission to found a hospital in the neighbourhood of the Castle of Wartburg, and there she established twenty-eight poor creatures, who had no home on earth, and no one to care for their wants. She visited them every day, carrying to them food and drink, and nursing them tenderly and lovingly as she could.

It was thus, that ere sixteen summers had passed over her head, that the King of Hungary's daughter spent her bright young life; it was thus that the love of earthly greatness died out of her heart, and there arose there that love of holy poverty, which was sanctified for ever by her blessed Lord.

Sometimes in her child-like innocence, the young Duchess would take off her costly clothes, and dress herself as a beggar, putting on a grey dress, and covering her head with a tattered veil, and would go amongst her maidens, and beg for a piece of bread, saying in words that were indeed prophetic of the fate that was in store for her: "This is how I shall walk when I am poor and miserable for Christ's sake." Well, indeed, might the saintly Bishop of Geneva say of her, the depths of whose simple, yet most loving nature, he above all men, perhaps, could best appreciate even at the distance of more than three hundred years: "Oh, my God, how poor this princess was in her riches; how rich in her poverty!"

CHAPTER V.—1221.

Elizabeth advances still further in the path of Perfection — Her
obedience to the rules of the Church — Her reverence for the
Blessed Sacrament — Her sorrow when, on one occasion, she
allowed the thought of earthly love to come between her and
her crucified Lord.

DAY by day the young Duchess advanced in the
path of Christian perfection. The love which had
been the chief characteristic of her saintly patron,
"the beloved disciple," grew and overflowed in the
heart which, in all the freshness of youth, had been
given to God; and that strange. humility, which
had so graced her childish years, sank more deeply
into her soul as time passed on. Loving all around
her, better than she loved herself, she loved God
first, and before all else. She trusted in Him, with
simple, child-like faith, whilst she obediently followed
every precept and command of the Church. In
the Holy Sacraments she found her greatest help
and comfort. She communicated frequently, but
always with fear and respect, mingled with reverential
love, for she knew what that blessing was, which
came to her in the sacred Eucharist. Whenever
she heard the sweet tones of the Chapel bell, calling

the faithful to keep the Church's hours, she would fly thither with girlish delight; and with outward gesture of reverence, and inward purity of soul she would worship and adore her Lord and Saviour. She carefully observed all days of obligation; and no words can tell the mingled piety and fervour and veneration with which she commemorated that holiest week in the Church's year, when the sad and dolorous tale of the Passion of Jesus is told to those souls for Whom He bore all these things. Already we have seen how on Maundy Thursday Elizabeth washed the feet of twelve lepers; and having done this, she would assume the dress of a beggar, and with bare feet she visited the different churches of the neighbourhood, walking many miles in her lowliness and humility. Then when night came, she knelt before a representation of the Divine Agony, and thus in prayer and contemplation waited for the dawn of that most solemn day, when all was indeed " finished,"— the sacrifice of love completed. On Good Friday morning she would say to her attendants, " This is a day of humiliation for all of us, I forbid any one of you to show me the smallest respect;" and afterwards she provided herself with some little packets of incense and linen, and some small tapers, and clad in the simple garb she had worn the day before, she would once more visit the churches, and leave her poor little offerings before each altar, then she

would go into the square of the town of Eisenach and
distribute her alms amongst the vast crowd that
thronged around her.   There were those at her
husband's Court, who marvelled at the poor offerings
the young Duchess made on that solemn day in the
house of God, but this like all else was a part of
her wondrous humility; the heavenly instinct which
guided every action of her life told her, that to be
humble on the day of her Lord's Agony, was to keep
that day with greatest honour to Him.   It was a part
of her nature to be generous and lavish in all things;
and it was a great sacrifice to offer so little, to curtail
her gifts to the level of the poor around her, who
had naught else to "lend to the Lord."   During the
Rogation Days, which at this period were celebrated
with all kinds of worldly festivities, Elizabeth, clad
in humble garb, bare-headed and bare-footed, took
her place in church amongst the beggars, and walked
with the poorest of her subjects in the procession
which followed the relics of the Saints and the Cross
of the Saviour; "for," says an old historian, "all her
glory was in the Cross and Passion of Christ; the
world was crucified for her, and she was crucified
to the world."

On one occasion we are told, that during a solemn
celebration of Mass on a high festival, Elizabeth
for an instant forgot the holiness of the Sacrifice, and
allowed her eyes to rest upon Louis, who was kneeling

by her side. Her heart was full of love, as she gazed
upon his rare beauty, and thought with joy of his
many noble qualities, which rendered him so dear
to all, dearest of all to her—his cherished wife.
Then she turned towards the Altar, just as the priest
elevated the consecrated Host for the adoration of
the people, and it seemed to her as though he held in
his hands her crucified Lord, and the crimson Blood
was flowing from His Sacred Wounds. She knew
then how great was the sin of which she had been
guilty, in forgetting, even for an instant, the Divine
Spouse of her heart, and she prostrated herself to
the earth, and wept bitterly, and asked God to pardon
her. Her husband accustomed to see her thus rapt in
devotion, left the church, thinking that she would
soon follow him. The hour of dinner arrived, the
guests assembled, and still the Duchess did not appear,
and Louis went to seek her. He found her where
he had left her, bowed before the Altar in sorrow
and in penitence. "Dear sister," he said gently,
"why do you not come to dinner; why have you
kept us waiting for so long?" At his voice she raised
her streaming eyes to his face, but could find no words
in which to answer him. "Dear sister, why these
bitter tears; will you not tell me your trouble?"

She poured out her tale of sorrow and of self-
reproach, and at the simple recital the Duke's tears
were mingled with hers, and he said "Let us trust

in God, dear sister; I will help you to repent, and
to become better than you are." And then, seeing
that she could not join his guests that day, Louis
wiped away his tears and went back to the festive
board, to apologise for his wife's unavoidable absence.
Elizabeth still knelt on in the church, and wept
and prayed, and asked pardon for her fault. And
surely those bitter tears, that "blood of the soul,"
as S. Augustine calls them, were carried by Angels
to the feet of the Father of Mercies, and looked
upon by Him as the precious fruits of repentance
and holy love, to be set as shining pearls in the
gates of Paradise.

CHAPTER VI.—1221.

S. Dominic of Guzman, and S. Francis d'Assisi — The rule of the
Third Order of S. Francis —The Franciscans in Eisenach —
Elizabeth's veneration for the Saint of Assisi —She joins the
Penitents of the Third Order of S. Francis — The Saint's
present to the young Duchess — Maître Conrad of Marburg is
appointed Elizabeth's spiritual director by the Pope — The
rule of life which this good man gave to his spiritual daughter.

For some years before this period, the eyes of all the
faithful in Europe were turned towards the founders of
two new great Orders in the Church, those of S. Dominic
of Guzman, and of S. Francis d'Assisi. The story of
the lives of these great saints is familiar to us all ; but
one fact, seeming strangely to connect S. Francis with
" the dear Elizabeth," must not be passed unnoticed.
When, in 1206, the star shone over the place of the
Princess of Hungary's birth, the star of Divine Light
also passed into the heart of the young and gay
Italian, the Saint of Assisi. The wild and reckless
but most generous youth was in that year turned from
darkness to light—from the power of Satan to the
truth of God. He began that life of voluntary poverty,
the fire of which was to spread and kindle through the
whole Christian world ; and men and women longed to

give up home and country, and earthly love ; to leave
that state of life in which God had placed them, and
to follow the example of the gentle, blameless saint;
and giving up all they had on earth become poor, and
despised, and persecuted. S. Francis hardly knew
how to deal with such souls as these ; he saw their
intense yearning for a higher, holier life than that
which they could lead in the world ; and yet to separate
husbands from their wives, and fathers and mothers
from their children, such would be to break the sacred
ties consecrated by God Himself ; so he formed a third
order in his society, which already consisted of the
preaching brothers and of the Sisters of S. Clare, who
were bound by the triple vow of poverty, chastity, and
obedience ; and he ruled that those men and women
who joined this third order should live in their own
homes, and that if they were married the joint consent
of both husband and wife must be obtained ere either
took the solemn step. Then they were to try and
make reparation for all the wrong they had ever done,
and to be publicly reconciled to their enemies. They
were to dress in grey or some such sober colour, and
the men were to carry no arms, except in defence of
the Church or of their country. They were to renounce
as much as lay in their power all worldly gaiety, to
keep all the fasts of the Church with strictness, to hear
Mass every day, to communicate on all days of obligation, to say some special prayers, to visit the sick

brethren and sisters of the Order, and to attend their funerals. These rules had in them nothing of monastic rigour, whilst they associated the penitents of the Third Order of S. Francis, by a holy and sacred tie with those of their brethren and sisters, whom circumstances enabled to lead the life of poverty.

In 1221 a little body of Franciscans found their way into Germany, and encouraged by all they had heard of the young Duchess of Thuringia, they felt that no more fitting locality than the old town of Eisenach could be chosen by them in which to begin their work. They obtained from Elizabeth all the sympathy and encouragement they had expected; very soon she founded a convent for them, and built them a church in the capital, and one of their own brothers was chosen by her as her spiritual director. He remained at Eisenach, however, only for a short time, and then it was that Father Conrad, to whom we have already alluded, became the Saint's Confessor. An ardent affection for S. Francis took possession of her heart; his great humility, his love of poverty, his life of hardship all found their echo in her breast; he seemed to unite all the virtues which from her childish years she had so dearly prized, and which she had striven so hard and so successfully to acquire. She asked, and readily obtained her husband's consent, to join the penitents of the Third Order of S. Francis, and she was the first in Germany to assume that habit which after-

wards was worn by so many saints. The Saint of
Assisi heard of all the good deeds of Elizabeth, and
one day, when he was talking of the young Duchess to
Cardinal Ugolino (afterwards Pope Gregory IX.), the
patron of his Order, the latter advised him to send
Elizabeth some token of his love and esteem. "I
should like you," said the Cardinal "since she seems
imbued with your spirit to send her the same heritage
as that which Elijah bestowed upon Elisha ;" and so
saying he took off the old worn mantle from the
shoulders of S. Francis, and bade him send that to the
humble Elizabeth. The saint obeyed, and ever afterwards the young Duchess prized that old mantle as her
most precious earthly possession, and always put it on
when she prayed for any special grace. Afterwards
when she gave up everything in the world that belonged
to her, she retained her " dear father's " much valued
present. When she died she left it as a sacred legacy
to a dear friend.

Elizabeth had been married only one year when she
joined the Third Order of the Franciscans. Very soon
afterwards the Confessor she had chosen was removed
from Eisenach, and to her great grief she was obliged
to seek another. Her husband wrote to the Pope and
asked him to recommend a learned and pious guide for
his young wife, and at his suggestion it was, that
Elizabeth became the spiritual daughter of Conrad of
Marburg, whose advice in all things, as we have already

E

seen, she so unswervingly followed. This good man had renounced all worldly honours, all hope of advancement in the Church, and had given up his life to the poor. Mounted on a little mule he rode from one end of Germany to the other, whilst crowds followed him to listen to the words of wisdom which fell from his lips. When Elizabeth heard that Father Conrad was to watch over her spiritual life, she exclaimed: "Oh, poor sinner that I am, I am not worthy that this great saint should have the care of my soul; oh, my God, I thank Thee for Thy great mercy." And she tried to prepare herself for what she looked upon as so great a good, by additional fastings and prayers. When she heard that *Maître* Conrad, as he was always called, was approaching the Castle, she went out to meet him, and threw herself at his feet, saying: " My spiritual father, deign to receive me as your daughter in Christ; I am unworthy of you, but I beseech you, by the love I bear my brother, to have compassion on me." Conrad, who saw at a glance all the depths of Elizabeth's humility, could not help exclaiming: " O Lord Jesus, what wonders dost Thou work in those souls which are really Thine." All the Priest's zeal was from that time devoted to the culture of that most precious flower which he was to make fit to bloom in the Paradise of God. The depths of spiritual life brought out by such teaching developed with marvellous rapidity in the young Duchess' mind.

All thoughts of earth were crushed within her; her mind seemed ever dwelling upon the things of heaven. She longed to give her life to God, to let no human affection come between her and the heavenly Bridegroom she would fain have chosen; and yet her love for her husband was as deep and true and tender as it had ever been, and he in his turn tried to help her to the holiness for which she so yearned. Maître Conrad, putting aside, as was his bounden duty, all thought of her high station, sought only to look upon her as a spiritual daughter given into his keeping straight from God; and as she had voluntarily taken the vow of absolute obedience to him, he enforced that obedience with all the strength and firmness of his upright, unbending, somewhat stern character. One day he sent for her to hear a sermon. She had some visitors at the Castle, and could not conveniently get away; and Maître Conrad sent to tell her that he could no longer undertake her spiritual direction. The next day she ran to him covered with shame, and entreated him with many tears to retract his cruel decision, and to pardon her fault. She threw herself at his feet, and would not leave him until she had obtained his forgiveness; he gave it her at last, coupled with a severe penance, as a punishment of her disobedience.

The rule of life which this wise and rigid confessor gave to Elizabeth has been carefully preserved by the ancient chroniclers; it runs as follows :—

E 2

1. Patiently suffer contempt in the midst of voluntary poverty.

2. Give to humility the first place in your heart.

3. Forsake all earthly consolations and all carnal enjoyments.

4. In all things show mercy to your neighbour.

5. Have a perpetual recollection of the presence of God.

6. Thank Jesus, Who by His death has saved you from hell and death eternal.

7. Since God has suffered so much for you, bear His Cross patiently.

8. Dedicate yourself entirely body and soul to God.

9. Always remember that you are the work of God's Hands, and act so that you may live with Him in eternity.

10. Forgive your neighbour, as you would be forgiven by him; do for him all that you would wish him to do for you.

11. Always remember that life is short, and that the young die as well as the old. Aim ever towards life eternal.

12. Deplore your sins unceasingly, and ask God to forgive them.

CHAPTER VII.—1221-1225.

King Andrew of Hungary sends an Embassy to the Court of
Thuringia — Elizabeth's dress, and her reception of her
father's friends — The young Duke and Duchess visit Hungary — The story of Elizabeth and the importunate Beggar —
The new joy that came to the Husband and Wife in the birth
of Children — Elizabeth's dedication of her little ones to
Jesus.

Soon after Elizabeth's marriage, her father, the good
King Andrew of Hungary, sent an embassy to his
daughter's far off Thuringian home to see how it fared
with her, and whether she was really as happy as one
so good and lovely and innocent deserved to be, and
at the same time to invite her and her young husband
to rejoice his heart and cheer the short remainder of
the days of his life, by visiting him in his own
dominions. The Landgrave received his guests with
every mark of honour and esteem, and then it struck
him that Elizabeth had no fit garments in which to
receive these magnates of the Hungarian Court.
Anxious to see what she would do in such an
extremity, he sought her out in her own chamber, and
said: " Ah, dear sister, here are messengers from your
father come to see what kind of life you are leading

with me, and if you are really a Duchess in state as
well as in name. How are you to appear before them?
You are so occupied with the poor that you forget
yourself; you never will dress but in these poor clothes
which shame us both. What a disgrace it will be for
me when they return to Hungary and say that I do
not clothe you properly, and that they found you in
such a pitiable state; for now there is no time to get
other dresses made, such as would do honour to your
rank and to mine." Louis spoke with more than ordi-
nary irritation; but Elizabeth answered him gently:
" My dear lord and brother, do not thus distress yourself, for I have quite determined never to set my pride
upon my dress; I will excuse myself to these Hungarian nobles, and I will force myself to be so gracious
and affable to them, that they shall be more pleased
with me than if I were attired in the finest clothes."
She then prayed that God would make her agreeable
in the eyes of her father's friends; and putting on the
best things she had, she went down with her husband
to the great hall of the Castle to meet the Ambassadors.
She nobly kept her promise; she charmed every one
by her sweet, bright gaiety, and by her excessive
beauty; but to the great surprise of her husband and
his Court, and to the admiration of the strangers, she
appeared before them dressed in the rarest and most
costly silks, and wrapped in a mantle of azure velvet
studded with precious pearls. When the Hungarians

had taken their departure, Louis returned to his wife, and asked her how she had possessed herself of such gorgeous attire? With a sweet, holy smile, she answered him : "It is thus our dear Lord deals with His servants, when it so pleases Him."

The following year, 1222, the Duke took Elizabeth to the country of her birth, to which she had always looked back with such loving, tender recollections. King Andrew received his darling child with every expression of joy, and sent her and her young husband home, after some months, with words of fervent blessing, and laden with many costly presents. Soon after their return to Thuringia, Agnes, the duke's beautiful sister, was married to Henry of Austria ; and great fêtes were held at Wartburg in honour of the nuptials, to which all the chief lords and ladies of the kingdom were invited. One day the banquet was ready ; all had assembled but the young Duchess, and they waited for her appearance, but still she came not. Then the Seneschal entered the hall and told Louis the cause of his wife's absence. It appeared that as she was hurrying from Church to the banquet, a poor miserable beggar had stopped her, and would not let her go until she had bestowed an alms upon him. He was ill and weak, and nearly naked, and she told him she had nothing to give him, but that she would send him something from the feast. Still he would not let her go ; for Christ's dear sake he implored her not to leave him without giving him some token of her charity. Her heart was touched with a strange pity for the poor man; and hastily taking off her richly jewelled mantle, she threw it to him and went on her way, whilst the beggar wrapped up the costly garment and suddenly disappeared with it. "And," continued the Seneschal, "it is thus, my lord, that the good Duchess was employed; whilst you were awaiting her here, she was clothing the poor, and giving her cloak to a beggar." The Landgrave laughingly answered: "I must see what all this means; she will be with us directly;" and so saying, he left the banqueting hall. In the meantime Elizabeth had ascended to her own apartments; for to appear before her guests without the mantle, which was the necessary covering of those times, would have been an unpardonable breach of decorum. "My sister," said Louis, when he reached his wife's room, "will you not dine with us to-day? We should have begun dinner long ago if we had not waited for you." "I am ready to do as you wish, dearest brother," she replied. "But where," asked the Duke, "is the mantle you wore at church this morning?" "I have given it away, my brother; but it matters not, I will come dressed as I am."

Just as she spoke these words, one of her attendants appeared, carrying the mantle Elizabeth had given to the beggar, and which, she said, she had found hanging in the wardrobe. For an instant the young Duchess knelt and thanked God for His mercy; and then she joined the gay throng with her husband, and was the gayest and brightest of all that courtly assembly. But Louis was strangely silent and reserved that day, for he was thinking of all those wonderful gifts which God had bestowed upon his Elizabeth; he knew that it was a holy Angel who had brought back that mantle which she had given to the beggar; and surely the beggar himself was none other than our Lord Jesus Christ, Who had appeared to "the dear Elizabeth," as centuries before He had appeared to the holy Saint Martin of Tours.

In 1223 a new joy was given to the young Duke and Duchess; a little son was born to them, and was baptized by the name of his grandfather the good Landgrave Hermann. In 1224 Elizabeth gave birth to a daughter, named Sophia. This young Princess afterwards married the Duke of Brabant, and from this marriage are descended the princes of the house of Hesse. The Saint had two other daughters, the younger of whom was born after her father's death. Both these children were dedicated to God from their cradle, and became the Brides of Christ. When God had thus blessed Elizabeth, by sending her those little innocent pledges of married love, she did not, as was the custom of the day, rejoice in her new happiness by proclaiming a great feast, and gathering around her the princes and nobles of the land. No; her gratitude and thankfulness took a far different expression to this. On each occasion of the birth of a child, as soon as she was able to get about, she took the little one in her arms and left the Castle by stealth, clad in a coarse woollen garment, and with bare feet she walked to the church of S. Catherine outside the walls of Eisenach. The way was long and wearisome, strewn with sharp stones, which pierced and tore her delicate feet; but she went bravely on, and then when she had reached the church, she placed her child upon the Altar with a taper and a lamb, and said, "Lord Jesus Christ, I offer unto Thee, as well as to thy dear Mother Mary, this dear fruit of my womb. Here I yield it to Thee, my God and my Lord, as Thou hast given it to me—to Thee, Who art the Sovereign and the Father both of mother and child. The only prayer I make unto Thee to-day, the only grace I ask of Thee, is that Thou wilt receive this little infant, all bathed with my tears, into the number of Thy servants, and Thy friends, and give unto it Thy heavenly benediction."

CHAPTER VIII.—1225-1226.

The Landgrave of Thuringia leaves his home — His valiant
deeds and love of justice — He helps Frederick II. in Italy —
Famine in Thuringia — Elizabeth's great Charity and Faith —
Louis returns to his native land — Elizabeth's great joy —
Plenty once more in the land.

WE are now fast hurrying onwards to the close of that
happy married life, upon which we have dwelt in the
preceding chapters. The brightness had reached its
zenith ; all looked joyous and sunny enough ; no cloud
was on the fair horizon of S. Elizabeth's young and
loving existence. The earthly love that God had
given her was inestimably precious to her, but neither
husband nor children held the first place in her heart,
that was given in all its freshness and entirety to
Him from Whom all her happiness came ; to Him Who,
when all around her looked brightest, she saw with the
eye of faith, hanging on the Cross of Agony, bleeding,
dying, suffering for her sake.

It was in the year 1225, that something of sorrow
came to the loving wife, and with many a prayer, and
many a tear, she saw her brave Louis leave Thuringia
at the head of a vast army, and march to the banks
of the Elbe, on his way into Poland.

It was on the 15th of July, the day on which the early Church celebrated the dispersion of the Apostles into distant lands to convert the Gentiles, that the young Landgrave set forth to redress the wrongs of some of the poorest of his subjects, who had been robbed and defrauded by the soldiers of the Duke of Poland. Louis besieged the Castle of Lubitz, and gained a signal victory over the Poles, and then returned, covered with honours and laurels, to the home and wife he loved so well. At the close of that same year, however, he once more placed himself at the head of his nobles, and marched into Franconia; this time to seek justice for a poor pedlar, whom the Franconians had robbed of his pack and of his donkey, and had disregarded the safe conduct given him by Louis. The Prince, Bishop of Wurtzburg, sent ambassadors to the Landgrave, to know why he thus sought to enter his country. Louis replied, that he wanted to find a donkey which belonged to him, and which the Bishop's men had stolen. The donkey and the pack were immediately restored, and Louis returned to Thuringia, in triumph, whilst the poor people showered their blessings upon him, and thanked God, Who had given them a Prince who made all their joys and sorrows his, and who espoused their cause as warmly, ay far more warmly than he would have done that of the most powerful noble in his dominions.

These are but trifling incidents, hardly perhaps worthy of record, but they show the young Landgrave's stern uncompromising sense of justice. And in the years that were to come, S. Elizabeth loved to look back upon them; and she knew that he who had done what he could for the least of the brethren of the Lord he so faithfully served, had his sure reward in the far off land, whither God in His mercy had taken him.

Ere the winter of 1225 was over, Louis had crossed the Alps, and with his usual undaunted courage had helped the Emperor Frederick II. to subdue the insurgents in Italy; and Frederick, as a reward for his many gallant deeds, gave him permission at the Diet of the Empire, which was held at Cremona, at Easter 1226, to carry his arms into Prussia and Lithuania, and to conquer what he could of those countries. With all the enthusiasm of his ardent nature, the young Landgrave entered into the project, for his most earnest desire was to carry the faith of Christ into those lands where the darkness of heathenism still reigned. *Mais l'homme propose, et Dieu dispose*, Louis' wish was not to be fulfilled then; other events were crowding thick and fast upon him; bad news from home came upon him in the midst of his triumphs; and he hurried back to Thuringia and his Elizabeth, and in after years when he lay in his quiet grave, the work he had sought to do was done by others, and the banner of the Cross was raised in Prussia and Lithuania, by Louis' own brother Conrad, and the Teutonic knights.

The news that had come to the Landgrave of Thuringia was, that a terrible famine was raging throughout all Germany, falling most heavily upon his own fair country.

Everywhere there was dire misery; the poor people wandered far and wide in search of food, greedily devouring the wild fruits and herbs which generally served as provender for the animals, and when this failed, eating the carcasses of the horses and asses which lay by the roadside. Hundreds and hundreds of poor creatures, weary and worn and exhausted, laid themselves down in their despair, and died, far away from their homes; and the woods, and fields, and hedges were the death-beds of many a suffering one in those days of bitter trouble.

The tender heart of S. Elizabeth was deeply moved when day after day tidings were brought her of all these things; and her one thought was how she might help those who, like herself, were God's own children, whom Jesus had called brethren, and for whom, as for her, He had suffered and died.

She opened the gates of the Castle of Wartburg, and to the crowds that flocked in she distributed the money which she found in the ducal treasury. Then she gave the corn from her husband's granaries to the poor starving wretches, who looked upon her as an Angel sent them from Heaven. She kept nothing back ; in vain did the officers of the Court remonstrate with her, and threaten her with her husband's displeasure ; she only smiled her own sweet smile, and went on day by day giving to the people as much corn as was necessary for their daily wants.

But in spite of the numbers who flocked to the Castle, there were others, old men, and women, and little children, and some worn by sickness and suffering, who could not climb the steep ascent, at the top of which the ducal residence was situated, and for them S. Elizabeth ever showed the most tender compassion. She would not run the risk of depriving the others, by bestowing what they were to have, upon these. So it was her own food she took to them ; every day she went to the hospital she had founded at the foot of the mountain, and with her own hands fed poor infirm men, and women, and little helpless children, whom God had made orphans. She founded two new hospitals in the town of Eisenach itself, one under the protection of the Holy Spirit, the other under that of S. Anne. And here every morning and evening she was to be found, standing by the bedside of the sick and of the dying, telling them of hope when the short suffering should be over, bidding them seek help in the Sacraments of the Church. No office was too menial for her to perform ; what others shrank from, what her attendants recoiled at, she cheerfully undertook, although naturally she sickened at all sights of horror, and turned faint at the foul atmosphere in which she now laboured so cheerfully. Yes, *naturally;* but there is a help which comes to those who seek it, and the *natural* gives place to the *supernatural.* "When I stand before the Judgment-seat," S. Elizabeth would smilingly say, "and when God asks me whether I have served His poor, I shall answer, Yes, my Lord; so much so, that my maids and servants have often been sick at heart because of it."

Children were ever her especial care and delight. In one of her hospitals there was a ward set apart especially for the orphans; and it was the brightest spot of the day in all the poor little lives, when the beautiful lady came amongst them with her sweet voice and winning ways, carrying with her some little present for each of them; soothing their sufferings, ministering to their wants, and listening, with tears in her eyes, to the little voices, which in chorus called her "*Mutter, Mutter,*" as the tiny arms were thrown around her as though entreating her protection.

And when all was over, when the last rites of the Church had been celebrated within those hospital walls, when weary souls had gone from earth to the unseen world, the young Duchess would perform the last offices for those poor worn out bodies, would dress them with loving hands in grave-clothes, and

would stand in the little quiet churchyard, sole
mourner sometimes, at a beggar's grave, with a
white veil over her head, with many a tear
flowing from her eyes, with many a prayer
ascending from the depths of her heart, that light
perpetual might shine upon those weary souls, and
that they might rest in peace.

To the poor prisoners too, she appeared as an
angel of mercy; many a time paying for the
release of those who were imprisoned for debt,
dressing the wounds caused by the heavy chains
with which the criminals were bound, leading
them to repentance and hope, bidding them bear
their punishment with patience here, and ask
God to deliver them from eternal chastisement
hereafter.

And in all these good works she was simple and
natural as a little child, only thankful that she was
found worthy to do anything for that loving Jesus
Who had done so much for her. Often she would
stop in the midst of her labours of love, and throwing
herself upon her knees, say: "O my God, I cannot
thank Thee enough, that Thou hast permitted me to
assemble together these poor people, who are Thy
dearest friends, and that Thou dost allow me thus
to wait upon them." It is recorded that as S.
Elizabeth one day said these words in the hospital,
the poor people she was attending thought they heard

F

a voice which said, " Rejoice, Elizabeth, for thou also art the friend of the Most High, and thou shinest before His eyes as the moon."

On one occasion, when she was going to distribute food to some poor people, she found a much larger number assembled than she had expected to meet. She feared her provisions would fall short, and she prayed to God to help her in her trouble. She gave all she had into the eager hands that were stretched out to receive her bounty, and yet the food was never exhausted; there it was until all had been fed, and still there was some left. The barrel of meal wasted not, neither did the cruse of oil fail, for the prayer of faith had gone up to the same God Who had compassion upon the poor widow and her little son in the land of the Israelites of old.

In the summer of that year of terrible trouble, a great joy came into S. Elizabeth's life ; her husband came back to help and console her in her difficulties, and to do what he could for his poor starving subjects.

All through the land there was great gladness and rejoicing, for it seemed as though when their Prince returned to them some good must come ; he was so wise and tender, and true, surely he would help them now. He arrived at the Castle on a Friday, at the hour of nones, and was met by the officers of his household, who poured into his ear their complaints against his wife's prodigality. They told him how she had wasted the money from the treasury; the corn from the royal granaries; he seemed not to heed their words. "Is my dear wife well?" he said, "that is all I want to know, I care for nothing else;" then he added: "I want you to let my good little Elizabeth bestow as many alms as she pleases, and it is my desire that you should aid her, rather than oppose her; let her do all she wishes to do for God; so long as she leaves me Eisenach and Wartburg I am content. God will give us back all the rest, when He sees fit. Almsgiving will never ruin us."

Then he hurried forward to embrace his wife, whose joy at seeing him, after the longest absence from him she had ever endured, knew no bounds. "Dear Sister," he said; "what has become of your poor people in this terrible year?"

She looked up into his face, and answered gently: "My brother, I have given unto God what was His, and God has kept for us, what is yours and mine." And truly it was so; for after all that had been done, the royal granaries were still filled with corn: good measure was indeed given to her, "who had given alms of her goods, and never turned her face from any poor man."

When autumn came there was an abundant harvest in Thuringia, and the poor people went back to their homes, clothed and cared for by Elizabeth, carrying with them the pleasant memory of her tender parting words, and blessing God who had given them such a Duke and Duchess to reign over them.

CHAPTER IX. 1227.

The Crusades — Louis of Thuringia takes the Cross — How Elizabeth found out the trial that was in store for her — Her bitter grief — The Landgrave tells his people of his determination — The Passion-Play — The visit to Reinhartsbrunn — The scene at Schmalkald — Louis' last speech to his knights and people. The Parting between the young husband and wife — Elizabeth returns to Wartburg.

ONCE more there was happiness in the old Castle at the top of the mountain, once more the young husband and wife took sweet counsel together, and gave thanks to God for all the mercies and blessings of their past lives, and asked Him to be near them still, even as He had ever been, in the yet untried path of the future.

But although in Thuringia all was peace, there came from afar tales of warfare and of bloodshed, of Christian heroism, and bright deeds of chivalry, all mingled together in the history of the Crusades, in those holy wars which moved the hearts of all good men and true, in such a strange mysterious manner.

Cardinal Ugolino had ascended the Papal Chair, under the title of Gregory IX., and his first act was to issue a proclamation to all the sovereigns of Christendom, summoning them to enter on a new Crusade.

The Emperor Frederick II., fresh from his conquests in Northern Italy, vowed to set sail in the autumn of 1227 for the Holy Land; all was made ready for the expedition; pilgrims flocked in from all quarters. In Germany, in Sicily, and England, the word went forth that Jerusalem must be saved, the Holy City rescued from the hands of the Infidels. The glories of the fourth Crusade were still fresh in men's minds; the noble deeds of Richard of England were set forth now as incitements to fresh deeds of valour; the Crescent must be made to yield to the Cross, and all Christian nations and Christian princes must join together to fight for Christ.

Then poets spoke in thrilling language of the miseries of the land which had been watered by the Precious Blood of Jesus, and their words of burning eloquence rang through the length and breadth of the nations of Europe.

"We all know," cried the German bard, Walter von der Vogelweide, "how this holy ground is abandoned and left solitary! Weep, Jerusalem, weep, because thou hast been forgotten. Life is passing quickly away; death will find us sinners. It is in trial and danger alone that mercy is to be found! Let us go and heal the Wounds of Christ; let us break the chains that bind this country. O Queen of all women, lend us thine aid! It is there that Thy Son was slain. It is there that He Who was so pure allowed Himself to be baptized, purified for our sakes. There He allowed Himself to be sold, that we might be redeemed, He Who was so rich, for us who are so poor. There He died the death of agony. All glory be to Thee, Lance, and Crown, and Thorns. Woe to thee, heathens! God wills that His insults should be avenged by His chosen ones."

And in some such words too, did the Royal Poet of Navarre, Thibaut of Champagne, address his knights, saying :—

"I know it well, my lords, lay the words to heart— that those on this earth where God lived and died who do not take the Cross will enter Paradise with great trouble. Any man who has any religion, any thought of the Lord Most High, should seek to avenge Him, to deliver His land and His country. All will flock thither, all who love God, and the honour of this world, all who would serve God as He wills to be served. None will stay behind but fools and cowards. How blind are those, who all through their lives will not help God, and who forfeit all worldly glory. For that God Who died for us upon the Cross will say to those who stand before Him at the last great day, 'You who have helped me to bear my Cross will go where the Angels are. You will there see

Me, and Mary my Mother. But you who never did
Me any seryice, will go to the pains of hell.' Sweet
Lady! crowned Queen, Holy Virgin, pray for us,
and then naught can harm us."

The echo of such words as these found their way
into the quiet Court of the Landgrave of Thuringia, and
a strange, new purpose came into the heart of the
brave young knight. His uncle, Louis the Pious, had
fought with Richard Cœur de Lion in Palestine, and
had been crowned with laurels. His father-in-law,
Andrew of Hungary, had spent many years of his
life beneath the burning Eastern sun, fighting against
the infidels. Was it not his duty to give the freshness
of his youth to God, to tear himself from his home,
and wife and children, and fight for Jesus upon
that holy ground, where His Blood had flown for
sinful men? Louis could not decide for himself; he
sought the advice of Conrad, the pious Bishop of
Hildesheim, and having obtained his sanction and his
blessing, he vowed to accompany the expedition which
was to sail for Palestine in the autumn, and he received
the Crusader's Cross, which the Germans called "*The
Flower of Christ*," at the hands of the venerable Prelate.
But as he rode home to the castle, his courage failed
him; he could face dangers and difficulties innu-
merable, he was brave and fearless as a lion, but he
could not face his young wife's grief, when he should
tell her of the heavy trial that was in store for her.

She was expecting the birth of her fourth child, and
he feared the effect such a communication might have
upon her health. He determined to put off the evil
day ; to wait until the hour of his departure came,
and to let her enjoy those last few weeks of happiness
which were still before them.

He did not wear the Cross upon his shoulder, as was
the custom of the Crusaders ; he carried it in the pouch
which was suspended from the girdle he wore round
his waist.

One evening the husband and wife were alone, and
Elizabeth, in playful mood, unfastened the girdle,
which dropped to the ground; the pouch flew open,
and there the loving girl—she was then only nineteen
years old—saw the Crusader's Cross, and divined in
an instant the heavy blow that was coming upon her.
She did not speak nor cry. She only looked into the
face she loved so well, that was bent with such pitying
tenderness upon her, and she fell senseless to the
ground. The Landgrave sought to restore her to con-
sciousness ; and at last she opened her eyes, and in
loving, gentle words he tried to comfort her, and to
tell her the reason of his resolve. "It is for the love
of our Lord Jesus Christ that I am doing this," he
said; "you would not wish to prevent my doing for
Him what I should be obliged to do for the emperor
if he issued his commands to me."

Still she could not answer him, could not willingly

pronounce what seemed to be her own death-warrant; then at last, with many tears, she spoke: " Oh, my dear, dear brother, if it be not going against God's will, I entreat you to stay with me."

" Dear sister," he answered, " let me go, for I have vowed to God that I would."

There was a sharp, fierce struggle between earthly love and submission to the Will of God, and then Elizabeth answered: " If God has chosen you, I cannot keep you back. May He give you His grace to serve Him in all things ; I have sacrificed you to Him, and I have also sacrificed myself. That His loving care may ever be with you, that every blessing may attend you, shall be my constant prayer. Go, then, in the Name of God." Again there was silence, for the hearts of both were too full for words; and then they spoke of their children, and resolved that that little one who was yet unborn, should be consecrated to God in the life of the cloister.

There was now no longer any occasion for secrecy; so Louis assembled his subjects and told them of his decision ; he bade them remember that he laid no taxes upon them to enable him to carry out his enterprise ; he only wished to give unto the Lord a part of what he had received from Him. He called a council of state, and consulted with them as to the best means of governing his kingdom during his absence. He exhorted his ministers to govern his people with mild-

ness and equity, and to enforce justice between the
vassals and their retainers; and then struggling manfully for firmness, he spoke to them his farewell words:
" Dear brothers in arms, barons, and noble knights,
and you, my faithful people; you know how in the
lifetime of my father, of pious memory, wars and dis-
turbances reigned in this our country.   You know
how many hardships and troubles my father bore,
how many journeys he undertook, how many fatigues
he braved, to preserve his kingdom from complete ruin.
He succeeded in doing this through his courage and
generosity, and his name is renowned to all time.   But
to me, as to Solomon the son of David, God has
granted quiet and peaceful days.   I see around me no
enemy whom I need fear; if I have had some little
trouble in the past, I am now at peace with all the
world; thanks to Him Who gives peace to His people.
You should all acknowledge this great good, and
be grateful to God for it; for myself—for the love of
that God Who has bestowed upon me so many blessings,
to show Him all my gratitude for them—and for the
salvation of my soul, I have resolved to go to the
East to defend that dear faith of Christ, which is there
so cruelly oppressed, and to protect it from the enemies
of the Name and the Blood of Christ.   I shall take
this journey at my own expense, and at no cost to you.
I give into the Holy keeping of the Most High my
good and well-beloved wife, my little children, my dear

mother and brothers, my friends, my people, and my country, all in fact that I leave behind me, of my own free will, for the honour of His holy Name. I entreat you to be at peace during my absence; above all I ask the lords of the land to behave as Christians should to my poor people. And I beg of you to pray for me very often; to ask God to keep me safe from harm, and to bring me back to you in health and safety, if such be His holy Will, for before all else I surrender myself, and you, and all that I have entirely to His Divine Protection." Breathlessly did all the assembled people listen to the Landgrave's words, as he thus spoke to them of all he would have them *do*; and whilst he was speaking they noticed that his face shone with a strange, new light, even the light of that faith and love, which in those days burned in men's hearts, and which mediæval writers have aptly called the "*Mystery of the Crusade.*" Strong men wept when Louis' voice ceased, and sighs, and tears, and broken words of love, and promises that all his wishes should be fulfilled, showed how deeply all felt the departure of their young and beloved Prince.

Then he chose the officers who were to be intrusted with the care of his houselold, and those who were to be placed at the head of his provinces, and he specially commended his wife to the protection of his mother, his brother, and his courtiers.

"I am quite sure, said the treasurer, that the Duchess will give away all she can find, and will bring us to misery."

To which Louis replied, that he had no fear of that, "for God would replace all that she gave away."

Then the better to bring before the minds of his people what that great object was, which caused him to leave them for a while, and journey into that distant land, he caused to be represented at his own expense at Eisenach, a drama which brought forward all the chief incidents in the Life and Passion and Death of our Blessed Lord. The actors were chosen from amongst the priests ; and step by step the scenes, which had been enacted more than twelve hundred years before, in the far off country of Palestine, were placed before the Thuringians. They gazed upon the entry into Jerusalem, upon the Saviour of the world, standing all silent before his judges, upon the kiss of betrayal, upon the mocking and scourging and the thorn-crowned brow, and upon that last most bitter Agony, when the sun refused to throw its light upon that dark hour when the Lord was crucified. Now-a-days we are familiar with the Passion Play ; many of us have seen that thrilling representation by the simple peasants of the Ober-Amergau ; all of us have read how the scene, in its deep reverence and solemnity and beauty, goes home to every heart. If such be the case now, what must it have been then, when, the ground

so sacred to the memory of all this agony, when
the land upon which the crimson streams of Jesus'
blood had flown, was in the hands of the destroyer
and the Infidel? The enthusiasm of the people was
at its height, they showered prayers and blessings
upon Louis, and bade him God-speed.

But ere he left his native land he had another
duty to perform. He visited all the monasteries and
convents, asking the prayers of the monks and nuns,
and distributing his alms amongst them. His gracious
manner and kindly words won all hearts, and loving
benedictions followed him as he went on his way,
and holy men and women prayed for him before the
Altars where the Lamb of God was offered in perpetual
Sacrifice for the sins of the whole world. At Reinhartsbrunn, the monastery which he had founded, and
which was especially dear to him, the parting scene
was one of peculiar interest ; his wife, his mother, his
brothers, and his little children accompanied him
thither ; and when Compline was over, and the monks
passed out of the choir, the prince knelt by the side of
the priest who was sprinkling the holy water, and as each
religious passed he drew him down to him and embraced him affectionately, even taking the little choir-
boys into his arms and imprinting a father's kiss upon
each innocent brow. Nothing was heard in the quiet
chapel but the stifled sobs of those who were so soon
to lose the prince who was so dear to them ; and at

last Louis himself gave way to the sad forebodings which had come upon his young, hopeful spirit, he too burst into tears, and said: "It is not without just cause that you thus weep, my dear friends, for I know that when I have left you rapacious wolves will come among you, and with their cruel teeth will persecute and torment you. But I know also that the Most High, remembering my pilgrimage, will open to you the bowels of His Mercy, and from my heart I ask that He will do this, now and for evermore." They were the last words he ever spoke to them; but the pleasant memory of his farewell shone with many a comforting ray into the hearts of those poor monks in the dark and troubled days that were at hand.

From Reinhartsbrunn Louis and his family went to Schmalkald, where he was to meet the knights and nobles who were to accompany him to the Holy Land. From all parts of his dominions crowds had assembled to see the last of him; and on the Feast of the Nativity of S. John Baptist, when the Church puts before her children the great example of holiness and self-denial of the Prophet of the wilderness, Louis of Thuringia, strong and brave and resolute, tore himself from the arms of those he loved best on earth. To his young brothers' care he committed his mother, his little children, and his wife. The innocent little ones looked on with wonder at the strange scene. "Good-

night, dear father," they said in lisping, baby accents,
"a thousand times good-night, dear father, of the
golden heart."

It was too much for him to bear; he gently put
his darlings away from him, and turned to his weeping
wife. He placed one arm round her, and another
round his mother, and held his dear ones to him, as
though he would keep them there for ever, whilst the
hot tears, which would not be repressed, rolled from his
eyes down his manly sunburnt cheeks. Half an hour
passed in this fashion; then in trembling tones he
spoke to his mother: "My beloved mother, I must go
from you; but I leave you to the care of your two
other sons, Conrad and Henry, and into your own charge
I give my wife, whose agony you even now see." But
neither mother nor wife would quit that loving embrace; and every eye was turned to the sad picture,
and the crowds of nobles and peasants passed around
them weeping at the sight of those two women clinging, in their bitter grief, to him who was leaving them to
fight for his God beneath the burning suns of Palestine.

And most of that vast assemblage had a private grief
of their own, as well as that general sorrow for the
family of their prince. There were husbands, and
fathers, and brothers, who wore upon their shoulders
the Crusader's Cross, the "*Flower of Christ*," and who
had to leave those as dear to them as Louis' wife and
children, and mother, and brothers were to him.

So there they all stood, a brave, bright band of warriors, around that centre group, which consisted of their Landgrave and his belongings; Thuringians, and Hessians, and Saxons were all knit in one strange bond that day; the community of suffering had made them one with each other, and with their prince.

A few there were too, who had no ties to bind them to home or country, whose hearts were fixed upon the Holy Land, whither they were going, with no thought of earthly love to come between them and the glorious aim they had in view, who stood apart, true pilgrims and Crusaders, and burst into a glad hymn of praise to God, Who had thought them worthy to suffer, to fight, and even to die for His sake.

And so the songs of joy went up to Heaven, mingled with the sighs and sobs drawn forth from many a bleeding heart; and something of peace seemed to fall upon those mourning ones in that hour of trial, as they heard of the love of Him Who soothes every human sorrow, and sanctifies every human tear. The hour of parting came at last; the Duke gently disengaged himself from his mother's embrace, and passing through the crowds who sought to touch his dress, his hands, and to press near him for one last word or look, he mounted his charger, and placing himself at the head of the Crusaders, joined, with faltering voice, in the sacred songs which rose all

G

clear and joyous to the bright Home of the God
of battle.

Elizabeth was still to be with him for a little while;
she had craved so earnestly to be allowed to accompany
him to the frontier of Thuringia that he had not been
able to refuse her request; and so, side by side, with
sad and mournful hearts, the young husband and wife
set forward upon the last earthly journey they were
ever to take together.

The frontier was reached; but neither could speak
those farewell words which seemed surging like a
mighty wave over their hearts. Elizabeth went
another day's journey, then another; and now she
said she did not think she could ever leave him; she
must be with him to the end. But strength came
from heaven into the poor, loving soul; and divine
love triumphed at last over the intensity of earthly
affection. The Lord of Varilla, the son of that true
knight to whom Andrew of Hungary had all those
years ago committed the care of his darling child, and
who had so nobly fulfilled his trust, approached the
Duke, and told him that "the time had come when
the Duchess must leave him."

There was silence for a few moments as the husband
and wife were clasped in that last fond embrace; no
sound was heard but the rustling of the trees in the
summer breeze, and the sobs which rent those two
loving hearts, which must now be separated for ever

in this world. But even then, amid all their grief and all their agony, they thought of another life, bought for them by the boundless love of Jesus; and they knew that they should meet again, where sorrow and parting, and tears should be no more.

Louis himself gave the signal of departure; and then, taking from his finger his signet ring, he showed it to his wife, and said: "Elizabeth, dearest of sisters, look well at this ring, and see engraven upon the sapphire, the Lamb of God carrying His banner; let it ever be to you a sure sign and token in all that concerns me. Whoever shall bring you this ring, dear and faithful sister, and shall tell you that I am alive or dead, believe all that he may say, for it will be the truth."

Then once more he took her into his arms, and said: "God bless and keep you, my little Elizabeth, my sweetest treasure; may the most faithful Lord guard over your soul, and keep up your courage. May He bless also your unborn child; we will do with it that which we agreed upon. Adieu, think ever of our life together, of our tender and holy love; never forget me in one of your prayers. Adieu, once more, adieu, I may not stay away longer." Tenderly he gave her to the care of her ladies, and then he rode away, looking back until he could see her no longer; then he set his face towards Jerusalem, for there he knew he should find peace.

They carried his poor young wife to her desolate home at Wartburg; and there she changed her royal attire for those sombre garments of widowhood, to which, ere many months had passed, she had so sad a right.

CHAPTER X.—1227.

The last hours of Louis of Thuringia — His dying commands to his knights — The vow they took before they embarked for the Holy Land.

WE can imagine how, in the long dreary days that followed her husband's departure, S. Elizabeth prayed, as he had bade her do, for his safety—prayed with all the intense fervour of her nature, that God would keep him safe from all harm. And the prayer was answered, as all fervent, holy prayers are ; although, not as in her blindness, the young Duchess would have asked that they might be. Louis was indeed watched over, and taken to the haven where he would be—taken from all earth's weariness—" to where God giveth His beloved sleep." The brave, courageous soldier was not allowed to fight for His Lord on earth ; he laid down his arms at the Foot of the Cross, and dwelt for ever with Jesus in the Paradise of Rest.

Louis at the head of his brave, bright band of warriors, passed through Franconia, Suabia, and Bavaria, crossed the Tyrolean Alps ; and traversing Lombardy and Tuscany, at length reached Apulia, where the Emperor had already assembled a powerful army of nearly sixty thousand men. The August sun shone with fearful intensity upon the fair Italian plains; the heat was such, it is said, as might have melted solid metal. Fever broke out amongst the Crusaders, and delayed their embarkation. But the Emperor and the Landgrave determined upon leaving the sick to follow when they could, and after solemn prayers and Sacraments prepared to set sail from Brindisi.

Ere Louis set foot upon the vessel which was to carry him to Palestine, he was seized with a shivering fit, and afterwards was in a burning fever. He battled manfully against his weakness; he struggled to throw off the terrible lassitude which oppressed him; but at the end of three days the Emperor landed at Otranto, where the Empress was, saying that he could not bear the inconvenience of the journey by sea. The Landgrave of Thuringia landed also, and went with his accustomed chivalrous courtesy to pay his respects to the Empress; and now the fever came on with renewed violence, and when he returned to the ship he was obliged to succumb to it. The malady now made fearful strides, and soon all hope was at an end; it was evident to all that the brave young prince could never get over it. He was the first to see his danger. He called his courtiers around him and told them that his end was very near; he made his will, he talked of his wife and of his children, but there was no regret

in his tone; no wish to stay a little longer on earth.
The faithful, obedient soldier knew that his last orders
had come, and was ready and willing, and glad to
obey. Death had found him willing to bear all hardships for his Lord—to fight for Him with his latest
breath. He was thankful that it was so; and the
thought of the joy to which he was going—of the Love
which was to be his for ever, took away the sting of
the grave from those last, sad, suffering days of the
young bright life. He knew that his wife and his
little ones would not be left alone; that "Our Father
in Heaven" would be with them; that the widow and
the orphans would be in safer, holier keeping than his
could ever have been. So without a shadow of regret
for the things of earth, he waited for the end, and
thought of the joy of meeting those he had best loved
on earth in the Paradise of Light.

He sent for the Patriarch of Jerusalem to bring him
the last Sacraments, and to administer to him Extreme
Unction. He made his last confession with that
wonderful humility which had characterised every
action of his life; in the presence of his weeping
courtiers he received his Viaticum, expressing his faith
and hope in the Mercy of the Crucified; his assurance
of pardon through the Precious Blood of Jesus.

He bade his knights announce his death to his wife
and his family, and gave them that ring which they
were to show his Elizabeth as a pledge of the truth of

their story. He asked them to think of him in their holy enterprise; and when they should have succeeded in it, he begged them to carry his bones to Thuringia, and to bury them in his own dear Monastery of Reinhartsbrunn, where he had already chosen his grave; and he entreated them, in the Name of God and of His Holy Virgin Mother, ever to remember him in their prayers; then he meekly crossed his hands upon his breast, and a smile of unearthly beauty was upon his face. " See, see," he said, "how white doves are hovering around me waiting that I may fly away with them!" And as he spoke these words he died, and went to take his place in his own true country amidst the saints and martyrs, and faithful soldiers of all ages of the Church.

His brave knights mourned him truly, for they felt that in him they had lost the light of their eyes; the enterprise in which they had embarked with such high hope and courage, seemed hard and difficult now that their leader was taken from them.

Some of them were not allowed to be with him they loved so well, in those last sad, and yet most blessed moments of his life; the news was brought to them on the wide seas, as they waited there expecting Louis' ship to follow them. They retraced their way to Otranto, and joined the others in a solemn oath to carry out all the wishes of their beloved Prince, if they should escape the perils and dangers of the Crusade. In the meantime they buried the brave young Landgrave with every mark of love and honour, and left his body to rest in that foreign land, whilst with sad and weary hearts they went forward to accomplish their vow. Some of them succeeded in reaching Jerusalem and praying at the Holy Sepulchre for the repose of the soul of their Prince ; and the next year (1228) the pilgrims returned to Otranto after that inglorious Crusade, which the treachery of Frederick rendered almost useless, and which ended in that terrible dispute between the Pope and the Emperor, which for a time involved the nations of Europe in deadly strife.

CHAPTER XI.—1227-1228.

Winter in the Castle of Wartburg — The sad news as carried to
Thuringia — Elizabeth is told of her husband's death — Her
utter desolation — Hope comes at last.

It was dreary winter time in Thuringia ; the snow fell
thick and fast upon the ground, the rivers were blocked
by the ice, and around Elizabeth's mountain home the
wind whistled through the bare, leafless landscape, as
though it would chant a requiem over those by-gone
summer joys, which for her at least were never again
to return.

And yet amid all this there was something of hope
and joy within the Castle walls, for a little daughter
had been born to the young Duchess, and the joyous,
child-like nature had revived under the influence of
this new gift, which she and Louis had received from
God, to be given back again as soon as might be to
Him, in that life to which they had destined it. When
the messengers arrived at Wartburg with the sad
tidings of the brave young Landgrave's death, it was
to his mother and his young brothers that they told
their tale. Then throughout all the land there was
bitter mourning ; there was one only amongst them all

who shed no tear—who smiled as she lay and gazed upon her baby, and thought of her Louis safe in a distant land with God's Angels watching over him. For the Duchess Sophia's first care had been to keep the sad tidings from Elizabeth until she should be somewhat stronger. She gave strict orders that, by word nor look, no one was to betray the dread secret; a strange new tenderness seemed to have come into the proud woman's heart for the gentle wife whom her son had so tenderly loved.

It must have been a hard matter to hide her own deep, mother's grief from those watchful eyes; but she succeeded in doing so; no suspicion of the truth was in Elizabeth's heart.

But at last there was no longer any need for delay; the time had come when the loving wife must know the trouble that God had sent her, and her mother-in-law undertook to tell her that she was a widow.

Some of the most trusted gentlemen and ladies of the Court accompanied her to the room, where the young Duchess lay upon a sofa; she received them with all her accustomed grace, thanking them for thus coming to congratulate her upon the birth of her child.

At last the Duchess Sophia spoke: " Take courage, my dear daughter," she said, " and do not be distressed at what has happened to your husband; for it is God's will, and to that you know we must all bow, even as he did."

Still no suspicion of the truth crossed Elizabeth's mind; her mother-in-law's calmness deceived her, or perhaps she could not think of life without Louis; could not believe that God, the God of Mercy, would take all joy from her at one fell stroke. The worst she could think was, that he had been taken prisoner.

"If my brother is a captive," she said, "with the help of God and our friends, he shall soon be released; my father, I am sure, will help us, and soon all will be well."

Then with faltering voice the Duchess spoke once more: "Oh, my dearly-loved daughter, be patient; take this ring which he has sent you, for a great sorrow has indeed come to us. Our Louis is dead."

"What do you mean?" cried Elizabeth; "I do not understand."

Again came the solemn words: "My daughter, he is dead."

And this time she knew it all—realized it all; there was no further need to tell her what that sorrow was, that had come to her so suddenly and unexpectedly.

She bowed her head upon her knees in the bitterness and abandonment of her utter desolation; then she clasped her hands tightly together, and in a voice strangely unlike her usually clear, silvery tones, she said: "Oh, Lord my God, oh, Lord my God; the world is indeed dead to me—the world and all its sweetness." She jumped up from her couch as though a sudden strength and energy had come to her, and running through the spacious rooms and corridors, she made the old walls of the Castle echo with the cry that told all the bitterness of her grief: "He is dead, he is dead." At last she fell exhausted and overcome with sorrow into the arms of her faithful attendants. They sought to speak to her of comfort, but she would not listen, only through her tears and sobs came the heart-broken words: "Now have I indeed lost all I had; oh, my beloved brother; oh, lover of my heart; oh, my good and pious husband, why are you dead, and have left me alone in my misery! How shall I live without you? Oh, poor deserted widow—poor unhappy widow that I am—what shall I do? May He Who forsakes not the widow and the orphans console me! O God comfort me! O Jesus strengthen me in my weakness."

It was the first ray of hope that came into the poor, bruised heart—that thought of God and of Jesus. It seemed as though already she had heard that loving, gentle Voice, which for more than eighteen hundred years has spoken out of the depths of His tender compassion to all those Whom He has seen fit to honour by laying upon them the heavy burden of His own sorrow. "What I do thou knowest not now, but thou shalt know hereafter." "In your patience possess ye your souls."

But once and again there came back to her whom the Lord loved so well, that He chastened and scourged her so severely, the violence of uncontrolled anguish. Times when no comfort came to her, when the waves of sorrow threatened to overwhelm her, when even that love of God, which had ever been in her heart, seemed to have gone from her. There was One Who suffered greater sorrow than we can ever suffer, Who was despised, rejected, forsaken by all on earth, and Who, ere the measure of His dire agony was accomplished, had yet one more trial—the most bitter of all to endure—the Voice of the Son of God went up from earth to Heaven in one great and exceeding sorrowful cry: "My God, My God, why hast Thou forsaken Me?" Can we wonder, then, that even from His chosen saints the Father seems sometimes to hide, for a little while, the exceeding comfort of His presence and His love? For "the servant is not greater than His Lord."

To human eyes it seemed as though no further sorrow could be needed to purify Elizabeth's soul; the trials of her childhood, the patiently borne sufferings of her early girlhood, had surely drawn her near to God; had detached her soul from all worldly things. Had not her whole life shown it, her works of mercy, her deeds of love? But He Who seeth not as man sees, in His mercy judged otherwise. There needed yet one thing more ere the loving, gentle girl could be numbered amongst His own blessed saints. Her heart must be wholly His; none other must share the love which He required from her. So He tried her with fiercest trial, until she was dead to all earthly joys and sorrows and then He poured upon her the dew of His Holy Spirit, and she arose strengthened and purified, and victorious, and earthly sorrow had no power to touch her more, for her heart and thoughts were surely fixed where the only true joys are to be found.

CHAPTER XII.—1228.

The fresh troubles that came into Elizabeth's life —· She and her
children are driven from the Castle of Wartburg — The walk to
Eisenach — The base ingratitude of the people — Elizabeth's
wanderings in search of shelter for herself and her little ones —
The Church at Eisenach — The Duchess' sufferings at the sight
of her children's misery — Her own deep faith and resignation — She sends her little ones away — The insults to which
she was subjected.

Scarce twenty summers had passed over Elizabeth's
life, when in the cold blast of that winter's day, all joy
seemed to be taken out of it, and hope and gladness
passed away never again to return, but to be succeeded
although she knew it not, by a greater joy and gladness
than any she had ever yet known, by a peace which
nothing should take from her. It is a sorrowful tale
which we have now to tell; it is the story not of a
loving and beloved wife, but of a suffering woman,
bearing dishonour and indignity, and counting all as
naught for the sake of the Master in whose holy Footsteps
she sought to walk. We shall see the soul struggling
in all things to bow to the will of God; the naturally
proud spirit bent and almost broken by the strange
mysterious power and glory of the ascetic life. And

then we shall see the end; we shall catch a far-away glimpse of the exceeding brightness which was revealed to her, when at last the Master came and called her. Then sight fails us; but day by day we recognise how near "the dear Elizabeth" is to us, when we say the Creed of the Catholic Church, and express our belief in the Communion of Saints.

For many days the people of Thuringia mourned for their loved prince; and the young widow in her great affliction had the comfort of human sympathy. And surely it is a comfort, in the dark hours of sorrow to know that others are weeping with us; it takes something out of the sting of our bitter grief to feel that the tears of others are flowing for us, that the prayers of others are rising up on our behalf to the Throne of Him Who wipeth all tears from all faces.

But soon all was changed; and scarcely had the first keen anguish died out of the hearts of Louis' people, than those same voices which had spoken such true words of mourning for him, such true words of compassion for the Duchess, uttered hard things of the widow, and turned against her who had ever been their truest and most sympathising friend. It was God's means of bringing His chosen Saint unto Himself; for surely the hardest trial that can come to us is the ingratitude of those whom we have succoured and cared for. We cannot wonder at it—we dare not

H

rebel—for Jesus went about doing good, and yet His own people crucified Him.

Louis' two young brothers, Henry and Conrad, were surrounded by evil counsellors, who took the opportunity of the Landgrave's death to carry out their own long-indulged spite towards their saintly young Duchess. Their first care was to represent to Henry (surnamed Raspon) that by the ancient laws of Thuringia the sovereignty must remain undivided in the hands of the elder prince of the royal family, who alone could be allowed to marry. If the younger sons wished to marry, they would be degraded to the rank of Counts of the Empire, and only be allowed to hold certain provinces as vassals of the Landgrave; thus Henry must at once assert his rights as sovereign, or they must for ever be set aside in favour of the little Hermann, Louis' eldest son. They dared not go so far as to counsel him to take the boy's life, but they pressed him to send Elizabeth and all her children from Wartburg, from Eisenach, and from all the other royal residences. When the young Duke grew up, they argued, he would be thankful to receive some small territory at his uncle's hands, in the meantime he must be sent far away with his " bigoted and prodigal mother."

Henry was not dead to all feelings of honour ; but he was weak and easily led, and ambition and the love of power held the first place in his heart. He listened to the voice of the tempter, and he persuaded his young brother Conrad to do the same. He forgot his promise to his dead brother; he was unmindful of the vow he had made to succour and protect Elizabeth and her little children, and he gave permission to his fawning, flattering courtiers to tell his sister-in-law that Wartburg, the scene of all the joys of her past life, must no longer be her home.

The messengers of these evil tidings found the young Duchess with her mother-in-law; the fellowship of grief had made those two strangely fond of each other's society in those days of their bitter affliction. They began by heaping reproaches upon their innocent victim; they accused her of having ruined the country, of having wasted the treasures of the State, and deceived and dishonoured her husband; and then, as the punishment for her many shortcomings, they announced to her that it was Henry's will that all her possessions should be taken from her, and that she should instantly leave the Castle.

In vain she pleaded for delay, and protested her innocence; her hard-hearted enemies stood unmoved before the sight of her grief, and only reiterated their stern commands. The Duchess Sophia indignantly protested against such cruelty; and throwing her arms around Elizabeth, said: "She shall stay with me; no one dare take her from me; where are my sons, I must speak to them."

But all was useless; the false courtiers would allow no chance of respite to the heart-broken widow. " She must leave instantly," they said; and with rude hands they separated the weeping princesses, whilst the Duchess Sophia, with tears and sobs, followed her daughter-in-law to the outer gate of the Castle. Elizabeth was not even allowed to carry away anything with her; but in the castle-yard she found her little children, and two of her maids of honour, who were likewise to be expelled from Wartburg.

It was a harrowing scene, one which no pen can ever describe, to which no painter can ever do justice. There stood the little orphan children, the young and beautiful widow, the aged mother, the little ones looking on in wondering silence, the poor old Duchess weeping and clinging to her loved ones. Elizabeth alone was calm, asking God's help to bear this new and most unexpected trial which He had been pleased to send her. Once more the Duchess Sophia pleaded against the stern decree, and asked to be allowed to see her sons Henry and Conrad, being sure, she said, that they would not resist her entreaties. She was told that they were out; the truth was, they had agreed to remain in hiding whilst the cruel mandate was executed, fearing lest the tears and prayers of their mother and their sister-in-law might move them from their stern purpose, and so draw upon them the displeasure of their wicked advisers.

The last moment came; the old Duchess gave way to the most violent grief and despair; the sorrow she had felt at her elder son's death was naught in comparison to the affliction that now had fallen upon her— to the shame that this conduct of her younger sons brought down upon her grey hairs; for she could give thanks for her Louis, her noble, gallant boy, safe and at rest; but in thinking of Henry and Conrad, cruel, perjured, disgraced, by their own fault, there was nothing but misery and wretchedness.

The heavy gates of the castle closed with an ominous clang, the old Duchess was left alone to weep, more for the living than for the dead, and Elizabeth, the King's daughter, the Duke's widow, was driven from the gates of her home, with her helpless children, and her two faithful attendants into the cold of that piercing winter's day.

There was no one to say one pitying word to her, no noble chivalrous knight to stand up and defend the cause of the oppressed lady.

Carrying her baby in her arms, followed by her three other children and her maids of honour, Elizabeth descended the steep and rugged path, down which she had so often hurried to the relief of the sick, and the poor and the afflicted; and the pitiless wind blew fiercely around her, and the snow beat into her lovely face, as she pursued her way bravely and courageously, in a strength not her own, and at last entered the town of Eisenach, where once all hearts had blessed her for her kindness and her charity. Perhaps she hoped to find some comfort there; perhaps she thought that some of those for whom she had done so much would help her in this her extremity. She could not yet realize the full measure of her desolation, could not understand that such base ingratitude, as that which she was so soon to experience, could exist on God's earth. When at last she did know it, when it came upon her in all the depth of unutterable woe,—comfort, God's own comfort, came with it. For Elizabeth remembered Him Whose whole life was spent in one long act of self-sacrifice; Who went about doing good, healing the sick, cleansing the lepers, raising the dead; and yet He was cast out of the synagogues, He was put out of the cities, " He came unto His own, and His own received Him not." And when the Duchess of Thuringia thought of what cruel man had done to the Incarnate God, she ceased to marvel at the ingratitude of those on whom she had bestowed so many benefits, and only rejoiced in the suffering that seemed to bring her nearer to her Lord.

Yes, she journeyed on to Eisenach in the cold of that winter's day, her little children following her in tears, her baby clasped to her breast, and she knocked at door after door, and sought in vain for admittance,

but none would take her in, for the Landgrave Henry
(or rather his wicked courtiers) had already issued
orders that whoever should receive Elizabeth or
her children, would incur his severest displeasure ;
and the people in their fear obeyed him, and were
guilty of the great sin of base ingratitude.

At last Elizabeth reached a miserable wayside tavern,
and there she almost forced the landlord to take
her in, declaring that an inn was open to all, and
that none dared thrust her from the shelter of that
poor door. " They have robbed me of all I had
in the world," she said, " there is nothing left for
me but to pray to God." The man, moved by some
strange feeling of compassion, gave the Duchess
of Thuringia a place in a shed where he kept his
domestic utensils, and where his pigs generally found
their night's lodging. He drove the animals out,
to make room for the royal lady and her helpless
little ones, and there, weary and tired, they lay down,
and the children slept, whilst the mother watched
and prayed, and a strange joy came into her heart.
At midnight she heard the Matin bell sound through
the clear still air from the chapel of that Franciscan
monastery which she had founded during the life
of her husband. She rose hurriedly, awoke her
children, and made her way thither ; and when the
office had been said, she asked that a *Te Deum*
might be sung, in order to thank God for those

troubles which He had sent her, and which brought
her so much nearer to Him.　The solemn joyous
strain ascended to heaven through the darkness of
that night of human anguish; and on to the end
of her life the echoes of that song of praise resounded
in Elizabeth's heart; she was ever giving thanks for
the sorrow that God had found her worthy to suffer.
In the bright days of her once happy life—that life
that now seemed so very far away—we have seen
how she had loved at the midnight hour to meditate
upon the birth of the Holy Child in the cold manger of
Bethlehem; now she was bearing ever so little for
Him; and, oh! what happiness it was, what joy and
peace unutterable.　"O Lord," she said, "Thy
holy Will must be done; yesterday I was a duchess,
rich and powerful, with broad lands and fair castles;
to-day I am a beggar, and no one will give me shelter.
O Lord, if in the days of my sovereignty I had
done more for Thee; if I had bestowed more alms,
performed more deeds of love, how happy should I
be now; but unfortunately I did so little for Thy
honour and glory."

For herself she was indeed thankful and resigned.
But there are some natures, the best and most unselfish,
to whom the keenest trials come in witnessing the
sufferings of others; for themselves they can bear
all; for those they love they are anxious and impatient;
and yet His Will must be done in all things; we

must not choose *how* we would suffer. Now the hardest of all sorrows was to be Elizabeth's portion. Around her in the chapel sat her little ones—the children God had given to her and her dead Louis—who, until yesterday, had been nursed in the lap of luxury, who hardly knew what it was to be denied anything they asked. They were cold and hungry enough, poor things, and they asked their Mother for warmth and food, and she could not give it them. Truly a sharp and bitter sword pierced through the Mother's heart, as the plaintive baby voices rose in something of a murmuring chorus, through the silence and stillness of the chapel. She cried aloud in her woman's agony; "I deserve to see them suffer; I repent bitterly of all my sins; my children were born princes and princesses, and now they are starving, and no bed even of straw is to be found for them; my soul is pierced with anguish on their account; for myself Thou knowest, oh my God, that I am not worthy to be promoted by Thee to the grace of poverty."

There seemed to be no answer to the mother's prayer; she must suffer yet a little while in God's own way, and His ways are not our ways. The long, weary hours of the night dragged on, and the cold grey dawn of the winter's morning stole into the chapel, and still that little group remained there, still the hungry, worn-out children prayed to be

taken home.　At last Elizabeth could bear it no
longer ; and once more the sad little procession went
on its way, back into the town of Eisenach, through
the streets where once the royal lady had bestowed
her alms with such liberal hand, where she had
spoken such words of comfort to many a suffering
one out of the depths of her loving heart; to and
fro she wandered, but none would open their doors
to her, until at last she came to the miserable lodging
of a poor Priest, who at some time or another had
been one of the many recipients of her bounty; he
could not turn her away, he had little enough to
offer, but what he had, was at her service; he prepared
beds of straw for her and for her children, and that
was all he could do.　Elizabeth was very grateful
to the good man ; and when she had seen her tired
children laid upon the poor couch which the Priest
had made ready for them, she once more went out
into the streets, and then she pledged the jewels
which she had worn when she was turned out of
the castle, and carried home some food to her almost
starving little ones.　But even the poor shelter of
the Priest's house was considered too good for her by
her stern, relentless enemies ; she was ordered to take
her children to the house of one of the courtiers,
who had always been her most rigorous persecutor;
and fearing that if she disobeyed, her darlings' lives
might be in danger, she quitted the only friendly

roof that had covered her and those she loved so
dearly, from the wind, and rain, and snow, and
went where she was bidden to go. Here fresh
indignities awaited her; she and the little ones were
shut up in a narrow, miserable little room, whilst
all food and all means of warmth were denied them,
and insult and obloquy and scorn were heaped by the
lord of the castle, and his wife, and attendants upon
the innocent head of the saintly young Duchess. One
night she spent within those inhospitable walls,
praying for herself and for her children , then in
despair at the sight of their sufferings, she determined
at all risks to leave the place, and once more to go
to the poor wayside inn, which was the only place
of refuge her enemies did not seem to grudge her.
Ere she left the castle she said, " I thank you, O
walls, that have protected me and mine this night,
as best you could, from the wind and the rain. I wish,
from the bottom of my heart, that I could thank your
master, but that I cannot do." So she and her
children and her faithful attendants, were again
located at the poor tavern; but the greater part
of Elizabeth's time, both during the day and also
during the cold dark nights, was spent in one or
other of the churches of Eisenach. " From these
at least," she said, " none dare chase me away; for they
belong to God, and God alone is my Host." But even
amid all her faith and love, her sorrows and trials

seemed to multiply; the children pined beneath the cold and hunger, to which they were so unaccustomed; and when at last friends from a distance, whom she could thoroughly trust, offered to take them from her, the poor mother's breaking heart was forced to acknowledge that so it must be, if she would save their lives. She had always dearly loved all children. When a child herself, she was never happy except when she was bestowing some gift upon her little companions; and as she grew older we have seen how little friendless orphans were her especial care and delight, how those little ones, who had lost their parents, had loved to call the beautiful lady by the sweet name of " Mother." And now she, in whose breast was implanted with special intensity that sweet and sacred tie, which was made most holy by the mutual love of the Virgin Mother and her loved Son, was to give up the last of all human consolations, was to surrender her children at the bidding of the Heavenly Father There was a double motive in accepting the sacrifice ; she knew it was for their good, but she knew also that it was necessary for her that her treasures should be given up, for the sight of their sufferings seemed the one thing that chained her to earth, that made her inclined to murmur at the will of God.

There was a struggle deep and intense, such as only a mother's heart can know; and then S. Elizabeth meekly bowed her head, and her little ones were taken from her one by one, and hidden from their enemies in some far away corner of their dead father's dominions.

Now she had only to think of herself; she knew that her darlings were safe, and she could bear anything that God might see fit to send her. Although she could hardly supply her own daily wants, she could not bear to partake of a meal which was not shared by some one more wretched than herself. She had parted, for her children's sake, with the few treasures with which she left Wartburg; now she took to spinning, that she might earn enough to be able to indulge, in what to her was the *luxury* of almsgiving. And so the long, lonely days of that sad life passed away; and although her persecutors seemed to leave her alone, and to cease tormenting her, not one hand in Eisenach was stretched out to help her; not one pitying voice spoke to her in tones of kindness and sympathy. On the contrary, those she had helped in former days taunted her now with mocking words, and this added to the weight of her misery.

There was an old beggar in the town, whom the Duchess had loaded with favours and benefits, who was suffering from a loathsome disease, and to whom she had ministered with gentle, tender pity; one day Elizabeth in her poverty was walking through one of the streets, through which ran a little gurgling stream, across which stones had been placed for the convenience of the passers-by. The old beggar was coming from the opposite direction, and refused to make way for the Duchess, and pushing rudely past, threw her into the muddy water. "There, " he cried, " that is your proper place ; you would not live as a duchess when you were one ; now you are poor and lying in the mud I am not going to take you out of it."

The Duchess only smiled, and got up as best she could, saying, " This is a reproach for the gold and jewels I once wore." " Then," an old historian says, " she went full of joy and resignation to wash her soiled garments in a neighbouring stream, and her patient soul in the Blood of the Lamb."

CHAPTER XIII.—1228.

The life of suffering and resignation — Elizabeth and her children
go to Kitzingen—Once moie there is peace — Elizabeth and
her children take up their abode at the Castle of Portenstein —
Her life there — She is persuaded to marry again — Her firm
refusal — Her pilgrimages to Erfurt and Andechs.

FROM henceforth the suffering life became a life of
prayer and sacrament, and communion with God. He
Who had asked all her love, to Whom she had so
willingly and gratefully granted it, now came to her
in His Church with all consolation, came to wipe
away the tears from her face, to reveal Himself to her
even on earth, a pledge and a foretaste of the bright
exceeding glory which should be her portion in the
heavenly Jerusalem. Day and night S. Elizabeth
knelt in the presence of her Lord before His holy
Altar; and then to her weary soul there came bright
visions of love, which sent a strange thrill of joy into
that true heart which had borne so much for Him, and
would bear all, even unto the end.

In after years when the subject of her canonisation
was under discussion, Ysentrude, the most true and
faithful of her maids of honour, who had been with
her through all her happy days, and was with her in

her sorrow even to the end, told of the ecstatic joy that
used to come to her royal mistress as she knelt in prayer
and communion with God. Very humbly the Saint
would tell her loved companion of the reason of that
bright and holy light, which those who saw her at this
time noticed on her suffering face. She had seen her
Saviour come to her, telling her that He was ever
with her if she would ever be with Him. And when
in bitter humiliation she confessed the many sins of
her life, He Who described Himself as the Lord Who
had pardoned the many trespasses of S. Mary Magdalene, appeared to her, and absolved her one by one
from the offences she had committed against Him.
Then she would see Him in His bitter Passion, bleeding, suffering, dying, for the sins of the whole world.

Again she would see that ever Blessed Virgin, into
whose keeping she had consigned herself when she
was but a little child, standing by her side, bidding her
learn all patience and meekness and gentleness from
the bright example of her dearly-loved Son; bidding
her know that no grace could be obtained without
continual strife and trouble—without unceasing prayer
and perpetual self-mortification. And when S. Elizabeth had listened to these things, and with the eye of
faith had seen the glory that should be revealed to her,
exceeding happiness was in her heart; and clasping
her hands upon her breast and bowing her head, she
would say those words which the Blessed Virgin has

left as an heritage to all God's Saints for evermore, whether joy or sorrow be their portion on earth : " Be it unto me according to Thy Word."

But although Elizabeth lived the life of poverty and hardship, which to her was the Christ-like life, there were those who had known her in the days of prosperity, whose hearts bled at the recital of her cruel wrongs, and who longed to redress them, and once more bring something of happiness into that young and chequered existence. The Duchess Sophia tried as hard as she could to soften the hearts of her sons Henry and Conrad, towards their unfortunate sister-in-law ; but all her endeavours were of no avail, and in her despair she turned to Matilda, Abbess of Kitzingen, the sister of Elizabeth's mother, the good Queen Gertrude, and told her of all her niece had suffered and was still suffering. The good Abbess lost no time in sending trusty messengers and conveyances to Eisenach, in order to convey the Duchess and her children to Franconia, that they might live with her in peace in her quiet convent. Elizabeth was but human, and her heart bounded with joy at the thought of once more seeing her darlings, of watching over them, and listening to their sweet baby prattle, far away from those cruel enemies who had so sorely oppressed her. The children were brought from their separate homes and given into their mother's arms, and then the whole party journeyed across the dark forests and steep

I

mountains which separated Thuringia from Franconia, and arrived safely at the convent, where the Abbess received them with much affection, and seemed to try to make her niece forget all the sorrows and indignities of the past, by paying her the honour which befitted her high station.

But even now when peace had once more come into her life, when once more she was loved, and obeyed, and waited on, as she had been in the old days, her thoughts seemed ever to be with the God Who had indeed been her very present help in trouble. She was gentle as ever to those around her ; thankful for the most trifling service rendered to herself or to her little ones ; but her greatest delight was to live as nearly as she could to the religious life, to keep the rules of the convent as strictly and rigidly as she could. Still it seemed that she was to find no sure resting-place on earth, for now in the midst of her newly-found happiness her uncle Egbert, the Prince Bishop of Bamberg, judged that the convent was not a fitting place for her and for her family, and that such a home as she had found there, in some way or another must distract the good nuns, and put out the arrangements of their quiet, holy, peaceful, daily life. She listened to the advice that sent such fresh sorrow to her poor bruised heart, meekly as she ever did when those whom she honoured and reverenced spoke to her of her affairs and those of her children. And then she obeyed her uncle's wishes; with great regret she bade farewell to that first peaceful haven whither she had been led after the many storms and waves of sorrow which had passed over her; and leaving her little daughter Sophia in her aunt's care, she went with her three other children to take up her residence in the Castle of Pottenstein, in the Bishopric of Bamberg, which Egbert assigned to her, and where he gave her a suite of attendants befitting her rank, bidding her rule over her household as she wished and thought best. Her faithful maids of honour Ysentrude and Guta were with her still; and here in her quiet mountain home, amidst the lovely scenery which was her especial delight, in sight of blue lakes, and snow-covered hills, and lovely valleys, and pleasant cornfields, Elizabeth lived with her children and her tried and dearly-loved friends, and praised God Who had made everything beautiful in His time, a faint dim foreshadowing of the exceeding loveliness of the City where no cloud or shadow of sorrow should ever reach, where no darkness could ever come, for " the Lamb is the light thereof."

Day and night, too, she prayed as she had done in the days of her bitter affliction, keeping all the Church's hours as regularly as though she had lived within convent walls, visiting the poor and the sick in the neighbourhood, ministering to their necessities, as she had done to those who had treated her with such base ingratitude in her own loved home in Thuringia.

Notwithstanding all the sufferings she had under-
gone, the widow of twenty years of age was fair and
lovely as a girl; she was strangely lovely, too, exiled
from those who ought to have been her friends, cruelly
treated by those who had promised to succour and
defend her; whilst the brave knights into whose care
Louis had consigned her on his death-bed, were far
away in a foreign land, fighting under the banner of the
Cross, and there was no telling when they would be at
home again, and able to fulfil their vow to their dead
prince.

Under these circumstances, Egbert of Bamberg
thought that the best and kindest thing he could do
for his niece would be to find her another and lawful
protector, and so he went to her and proposed to her
that she should marry again. It is said that the
husband he wanted to give her was one rich and
powerful, holding the first place in the Empire, none
other than Frederick II. himself. His wife, Yolande
of Jerusalem, had just died, and his most earnest wish
was to espouse the fair young Duchess of Thuringia.

With her accustomed meekness Elizabeth listened
to all her uncle had to say as to the advantages
of such a match; and then she replied that she
would rather be alone to the end of her life and
give herself up wholly to the service of God.

But the Bishop still pressed his suit; he bade
her remember all she had suffered, all she might

suffer again when God should take him from her, for he was an old man now, and could not expect to live much longer. Pottenstein of course was hers so long as he was Prince-Bishop of Bamberg, but when he was no more, even although he should bequeath it to her, who was to protect her from the foes who had driven her from her home, and who were even now ever seeking some opportunity of injuring her?

But even the fear of suffering could not change her resolution. An old French poet has told us how, in simple, respectful words, she answered her uncle's entreaties: "Sire, my lord and husband was one who loved me tenderly, who ever was my true and loyal friend; I shared his honour and his power; I had many treasures and jewels and worldly joys; but even then I always thought, what you well know, that earthly joys are worth nothing. This is why I wish to leave the world and pay to God what I owe Him—the debts of my soul. You know that all earthly luxuries only bring grief and torment and the death of the soul. Sire, I long to be with my Lord and Saviour; I ask of Him but one earthly boon; I have two children who are destined to be rich and great, and I should be very happy and very grateful to God if he loved me well enough to take them unto Himself." She here spoke of those two children who were not destined to the religious life; the little Sophia was already in a convent where she was ever to remain; her baby was, as we have seen, dedicated to God by its father and mother ere it drew the breath of life.

She did not then bring forward the vow she had taken during her husband's lifetime, that in the event of his death she would never marry again, but often she would speak to her maids of honour, who with her had taken a similar vow of chastity, and say: "I swore before God and my noble husband whilst he was alive, that I should never belong to any other man. I took this solemn vow in all purity, sincerity, and good faith. And now I trust in His mercy to defend me from the assaults and persuasions of those who would speak to me once more of earthly love. For my vow was not a conditional one, depending upon the will of my relations and friends; but it was spontaneous, free, and absolute, to consecrate myself entirely after the death of my beloved husband to the service of God. If against my own will I am given in marriage to any man, I will protest against it before the Altar; and if I can find no other means of escape, I will cut off my nose in order to make myself an object of horror."

But although she spoke with so much faith and assurance, she was greatly troubled by the importunity of her uncle; it seemed as though they still would chain her to earth and earthly thoughts, whilst her

one wish and desire was to mount heavenwards.
Once more she was overcome with sorrow, and then
again she found peace. She knelt before the Altar
of God, and asked the Father of the fatherless, the
Consolation of the widow, to be with her now as He
had ever been ; and with tears and sobs she sought the
Queen of Virgins, whom she had ever called by
the sweet holy name of mother since that sad day,
all those years ago, when they had told her that
her own dear mother was dead. And once more
fear went out of her heart, and holy peace reigned
there, such peace as God alone vouchsafes to those
who worship and adore His own sweet will. It is
at this time of Elizabeth's life that we hear of her
undertaking several pilgrimages ; going alone to
distant places, protected by God and His holy Angels,
to pray at the tomb of some departed saint, to ask
that some blessing might be given her from above, sent
to her straight from heaven. Such pilgrimages were
very common in mediæval times ; old men and women
and little children, and the sick and infirm did not
shrink from the fatigues which they might have to
encounter, whilst those who were strong and well
helped the others as best they could upon their way.
Twice the royal lady journeyed to Erfurt, a town
situated in the centre of her husband's dominions,
but belonging really to the Bishopric of Mayence.
It was celebrated then for its many sacred and

beautiful religious monuments ; in after days it became famous as the place where Luther pursued his studies, where first he put forth his erroneous doctrines and denied the holy truths taught by the Church from the beginning.

In a convent for fallen women, known then by the name of " Les Dames Blanches," afterwards occupied by the Ursulines, Elizabeth remained for many days in absolute solitude, and when she went away she left as a sole legacy to the nuns the little glass she had used in her simple meals, and which now-a-days is drank out of as each S. Elizabeth's day comes round by the young pupils of the community. She went, too, to visit the castle of her maternal ancestors at Andechs, which was situated on one of the high mountains which separates Bavaria from the Tyrol. This ancient and venerable pile had just been converted by Henry of Istria into a Benedictine monastery, and in after ages it became famous as the repository of the precious relics of many a saint of the Catholic Church, and for the miracles which were performed within its walls..

It was a lovely spot that was chosen as the site of that home of the good Benedictines ; from the mountain-top, far as the eye could reach, stretched out the fair hills, and plains, and sunny valleys of Bavaria, whilst, amid all that God had made so beautiful, there rose the churches and monasteries built by man in

His honour; some of them raising their lofty heads in the shade of the dark forests, others reflecting their glorious beauty of architecture upon the smooth surface of some blue lake. Many a pilgrim found rest and refreshment both for body and soul in those Bavarian monasteries; many a solemn vow was made there, many a blessing bestowed upon those who sought help from God. Often did Elizabeth gaze in rapture upon the lovely scene, upon the range of the mountains of the Tyrol, which hid Italy from view, upon the shining rivers which watered the whole land, so calm and steady in their onward course, telling how man's life should ever flow on towards the boundless ocean of eternity.

When centuries had passed away, and the errors of Protestantism had crept into the land, and the Church was robbed of her own, the Monastery of Andechs was desecrated by sacrilegious bands. In 1806 Maximilian, king of Bavaria, sold it to a Jew, having decreed that all religious property was to be secularized. But the Chapel was preserved, and in it a precious relic, which S. Elizabeth herself had laid upon the altar, a seal and a pledge that from henceforth her love should be given to God alone. It was the dress she had worn on the day upon which she was married to Louis, and at the same time she gave to the religious a little silver cross, containing the instruments of the Passion, which she had worn for many years about her person. And now in these days when Catholic truths are despised, and when men in their worldly wisdom smile at the simple faith of mediæval days, there are still found those who visit the place where S. Elizabeth prayed, and who kneel where she knelt, and ask God to give them something of the meekness and humility of the young Duchess of Thuringia.

CHAPTER XIV.—1228.

The return of the knights, bearing with them the body of the
Landgrave—The progress of their journey—Their arrival at
Bamberg — Elizabeth gazes on the mortal remains of her
husband — Her complete submission to God's Will — She
receives the knights and asks their protection for her children
— Their vow.

IT was now more than a year since the brave knights
who had accompanied the Landgrave of Thuringia
upon the Crusade which he and they had undertaken
with such high hope, had stood by their brave young
master's death-bed at Otranto, and had sworn when
they had fulfilled their Crusader's vow to carry his
bones back to Thuringia, and bury them in the Monastery of Reinhartsbrunn. The time had now come
when Louis' dying wish was to be accomplished; the
Thuringian knights had done all they could do in the
Holy Land, and now in the year 1228 they returned to
Otranto, and prepared to carry Louis' body back to his
native land. Elizabeth had just returned from Andechs
to Pottenstein, braced for whatever fresh suffering
might be in store for her by the consolations of her
pious pilgrimage, when she received a message from
the Bishop of Bamberg, begging her to hasten thither,

as the pilgrims of the Cross, with their precious burden, might be daily expected there.

The historians of the middle ages tell us how that sad procession traversed Italy and Southern Germany on their way into Thuringia. They had disinterred the corpse at Otranto, and found the bones white as the driven snow, a sign of the life of purity which Louis had led. They had placed the sacred relics in a rich coffin, which was borne along in a car drawn by the dead Landgrave's own valiant charger. Before the coffin was carried a silver cross studded with precious stones, a sign of the hope and faith of the departed, and of the consolation of those who mourned him so truly. At night they rested on their way, carrying the corpse into a church and laying it before the Altar, where the soft tapers gleamed, and the sacred heart of Jesus beat in very love for the living and the dead. Crowds thronged into the House of God to chant low requiems there, and to pray for themselves and for the noble pious prince who had been cut off in the flower of his bright young manhood; and each morning ere the body was taken away a Mass was said for the repose of Louis' soul, and an offering made by the knights with the same intention.

At last the day arrived when the mournful cortége reached Bamberg. The bishop and priests went out to meet it, the bells from every church in the cathedral

city tolled with solemn sound, funeral chants rose
soft and sweet into the air, in which the voices of
little children mingled with the sonorous tones of
the priests and the people ; never had anything so
solemn been seen, never had grief so real and true
found its way into every heart; the cathedral was
reached, and there the coffin was laid before the High
Altar, and all that day and all through the night,
the Office for the Dead rose in continued solemn strain.
The next day the watchers by the corpse witnessed
a scene which must have dwelt for ever in their
memories with something of soothing sanctifying
influence. The widow, accompanied by her faithful
servants Ysentrude and Guta, advanced up the long
aisles with eager yet half-timed steps, for she longed
and yet dreaded to see all that was left of him she
had loved with such passionate tenderness. All the
first grief had come back on that sad day, when
the stern reality of Louis' death *must* force itself
upon her. There are such moments in the lives of
all of us, when we stand in the solemn presence
of those for whom, if need be, we would have given up
our lives, and feel that they are gone from us indeed,
never more to speak to us, or tell us how dear we
were to them. And yet surely they are nearer than
they ever were before; they can love us better and
pray for us better, than they did when they were
on earth, for they are nearer Him Who died for us

all, nearer the saints and martyrs who are ever praying for us.

But when the coffin was opened, when Elizabeth gazed upon those loved remains, there was a burst of violent unrestrained grief; nature asserted its sway, human anguish triumphed for an instant and only for an instant, then the sweet comfort of Divine love re-asserted its dominion in her heart; earthly affection was vanquished for ever, as that long, loud, bitter cry echoed through the old cathedral walls, and angels carried it to the Mercy-Seat, and offered it as a sacrifice at the feet of the Lord of all love, and winged their flight back again, bearing with them the great gift of perfect peace.

The widow rose from that loving embrace which she had imprinted upon her husband's remains, then she dried her eyes, and kneeling by the side of the coffin she said in calm firm tones: " I thank Thee, O Lord, that Thou hast deigned to listen to Thy servant, and to fulfil the great desire that was in my heart once more to see the remains of my beloved husband who also belonged to Thee. I thank Thee that Thou hast mercifully consoled my afflicted and desolated soul. He offered himself, and I too offered him, to defend Thy Holy Land; I do not repent this sacrifice, although I loved him with all my heart. Thou knowest, O my God, how I loved this husband, who loved Thee so much. Thou knowest that I would have counted the delight of his presence more than all earthly joy, if it had pleased Thee to grant it me. Thou knowest that I would have lived all my life with him in misery, he poor, and I poor, and begging with him my daily bread from door to door, from one end of the earth to the other, if only I might have had the happiness of being with him, if Thou hadst but willed it, O my God! But now I yield him, and I yield myself entirely to Thy will, and I would not, even if I could, ransom his life at the price of one hair of my head, unless it were Thy will, O Lord!"

Once more Elizabeth leant over the coffin, once more she spoke loving words to those unconscious remains, then with quiet dignity she walked out of the church, and found her way to a little grass-grown cloister, where she begged the Thuringian knights, who had accompanied her husband to the Holy Land, to grant her a few moments' conversation.

They had known her deep love for Louis, they had witnessed the heart-rending parting between the young husband and wife, and they dreaded the sight of her grief now, fresh from that trying scene in the Cathedral.

They need have had no such fears; when she saw them she rose from her seat with all her old royal grace and gentleness, and bowed to them humbly, as though she would show her thankfulness for all they had done for her husband, and consequently for her.

Then she begged them to be seated, as she did not feel strong enough to stand ; and when she had heard all she most wished to hear, all the sad and yet joyful story of that peaceful deathbed at Otranto, she poured into their ears the tale of her many wrongs ; she entreated them in the Name of Jesus Christ to be the protectors of her poor fatherless children ; she cared not for herself, she said, only for her little ones, for Louis' little ones, she asked for help and justice at their hands. The Bishop of Bamberg confirmed all her statements, indeed told the knights much that she in her charity, had left untold ; and the story was greeted with a burst of intense indignation, whilst the Crusaders took a solemn vow to redress the wrongs of their loved Prince's widow and children.

At their head was the noble young Lord of Varilla, and they swore to recognise no other ruler, to own no other sway than that of the little Hermann, Louis' young son.

They proposed to the Prince-Bishop of Bamberg that he should confide Elizabeth and her children to their care, and that they should take the royal party into Thuringia with the body of the Landgrave. They vowed that they would not rest until justice had been done, and until compensation had been made to the Duchess for all the injuries she had suffered at the hands of her enemies. The Bishop consented to the plan, and at the first dawn of the next day he celebrated a Pontifical Mass in his cathedral, and when he had blessed his niece and her children, and warmly thanked those who had so truly promised to befriend them, he let them go on their way to the Monastery of Reinhartsbrunn.

CHAPTER XV.—1228.

The Funeral in the Monastery of Reinhartsbrunn — The Knights agree upon their course of action — The Lord of Varilla speaks to the Landgrave Henry — Henry's answer — The Royal family of Thuringia ask Elizabeth's pardon — Her humility and graciousness — The return to Wartburg.

THE little quiet Chapel of Reinhartsbrunn presented a strange scene on that day when the body of the beloved Prince of Thuringia was to be laid in the resting-place which he himself had chosen. All through the country the news had spread that the remains of Louis were on their way to the monastery, and that following them were the wife and children who had been treated so cruelly by Henry and Conrad. All classes were determined to do honour to him they had loved so well, to try if they could to make up to his fair young widow for all she had been called upon to suffer; so old and young, and rich and poor, and noble and simple flocked to Reinhartsbrunn, and tears were in every eye, and sorrow in every heart, when they thought of the bright brave warrior who had gone in his youth and strength to fight for God in a foreign land, and who there had met his death. Bishops and Abbots came to do honour to the champion

of the Catholic Church; to him who, had it been
permitted him, would with his latest breath have
defended the Lord's Sepulchre; and the monks upon
whom he had lavished his bounties, and of whom
he had taken so sad a farewell, walked before his
coffin, and sang solemn funeral chants and hymns,
broken by the tears that *would* flow, when they
remembered all his goodness, and his bright winning
graciousness. His mother and his brothers were there,
sorrowing for him they had lost; and the Church's
most beautiful ritual was employed, and rich and rare
offerings were made, and the bones were enclosed in a
costly shrine, and placed in a stone tomb, and raised
up before the people, so that all might gaze upon
the sacred relics. Those who had known and loved
the Landgrave of Thuringia, ever called him S. Louis
when they spoke of him, and the historians of the
age have handed his name down to us with this
holy prefix attached to it. But the Church never
counted him amongst her Saints, although he has ever
been considered the worthy husband of her whose
name has been held in highest reverence for six hundred
years, as one of the brightest lights of the Catholic
Church. Now the old chapel of the Monastery
of Reinhartsbrunn is in the hands of the Lutherans,
and the tomb of the Landgrave of Thuringia was in
1525 pillaged by the Protestants, who impiously
scattered the bones far and wide about the surrounding

fields.   The broken stone of the tomb is still to be seen,—a sad memorial of uncatholic irreverence, and uncatholic want of charity.

When all the sad ceremony was at an end, and the last prayer had been said, and the echoes of the last dirge still rang through the vaulted roof, the Lord of Varilla advanced to the Crusaders, and bade them remember the promise that they had made to the Prince Bishop of Bamberg, regarding the rights of his niece and her children: "We must now," he said, "keep the faith which we swore to our noble prince, and to our lady Elizabeth, who has already endured so many miseries; otherwise I think we shall merit the fire of hell." There was a deep and solemn silence when these words were spoken, and then the knights retired to deliberate upon the best course of action to be pursued.

They unanimously agreed at once to present themselves before Henry, to remonstrate with him upon his cruelty to his sister-in-law, to tell him that they had vowed to see her righted, and that with their latest breath they intended to fight for her and for her children.   Four knights were chosen by the others to undertake this difficult mission; the Lord of Varilla was to speak in the name of his companions; but each and all promised to be staunch and firm, and not to give in, in one single point, to the demands they had agreed to make.

They found the young princes sitting with their
mother, and the Lord of Varilla stood firm and brave
before them, although his voice trembled with intense
emotion, as he turned to Henry and said : " My
lord; my friends, and your vassals who are here
present, have deputed me to speak to you in their
name. We have heard both in Franconia, and here
in Thuringia, grave charges made against you, which
have troubled us very much, and made us blush to
think that such things could be done in our country,
and that our princes should have been guilty of such
impiety, unfaithfulness, and want of honour. Alas,
young Prince! What have you done, and to what evil
counsellors have you listened? What! You have
driven ignominiously, even as a fallen woman, from your
castles and your towns your brother's wife, the poor
desolate widow, the daughter of an illustrious king,
whom it was your duty to honour and to console!
In defiance of all sense of honour, you have given
her up to misery, and have let her wander about
as a beggar. Whilst your brother gave up his life
for the love of God, his little orphans, whom you ought
to have nourished and protected with the affection and
devotion of a faithful guardian, are sent away from
you, and obliged to be separated from their mother,
to save them from dying of hunger! Is this your
fraternal piety? is this the lesson you learned from
your brother, that virtuous prince who would not thus

have acted towards the meanest and poorest of his subjects? No: a rude peasant would not have been such a traitor to his neighbour, as you, Prince, have been to that brother who went forth to die for the love of God! How can we trust for the future in your faith and your honour? You know that as a knight you are bound to protect the widows and the orphans, and yet you it is who have outraged the widow and the orphans of your own brother. I tell you in all truth, such conduct cries to God for vengeance!"

The noble knight stopped at this point, overcome by emotion; the sobs of the Duchess Sophia (who knew better perhaps than any one else how well-merited were those bitter words of accusation) resounded through the room; the young duke, troubled and ashamed, bent his head, but could speak no word of reply; and then the Lord of Varilla spoke once more: "My lord, what had you to fear from a poor broken-hearted, desolate woman, alone, without friends or allies in this strange land? What harm could this saintly and virtuous lady have done you, even had she remained mistress of all the castles in the country? What will be said of us now in other lands? Oh, what shame it is; I blush to think of it. Know that you have offended God, that you have dishonoured Thuringia, that you have tarnished your own name, and that of your noble race; and I fear that the wrath of God will be drawn down upon this country, unless you repent before Him, unless you are reconciled to this pious lady, and restore to your brother's children all that you have taken from them."

The bold, brave speech was ended, and all marvelled at the temerity with which the Lord of Varilla had spoken; he to whom it was addressed remained standing in his place, his head still bent in shame and humiliation; but even then God was doing His own work, the Holy Spirit struggling within young Henry's breast was convincing him of the sin he had committed. He raised his fair, boyish, tear-stained face at last, and said very simply: "I repent sincerely of all I have done; I will never again listen to the advice of those who thus counselled me; restore to me your confidence and your friendship; I will do all that my sister Elizabeth requires of me; I give you authority to dispose of my life and my possessions for her benefit. Yet," he added in a lower tone, "if all Germany belonged to her nothing of it would remain in her possession; she would give all away for the love of God."

Varilla only heard, or only heeded the first part of the speech. "It is well," he said joyfully; "it is the only way of escaping the vengeance of God." Then he and the other knights hurried to tell Elizabeth of the success of their interview, and to say that Henry's most earnest wish was to be reconciled to her.

But when they began to tell her of the conditions

she must impose upon him, she answered almost with impatience: " I do not want his castles, nor his lands, nor his towns; I want nothing that can in any way disturb or distract my thoughts; but I should be very grateful to my brother-in-law if he would give me the money that is due to me from my marriage-portion, so that I may be able to spend it for the salvation of my beloved husband and for my own."

The knights knew well from past experience that it was useless to reason with her, so they went and brought Henry and his mother, and Conrad to her, in order that the desired reconciliation might not be delayed.

With tears and sobs the young Duke asked Elizabeth to forgive him all the wrong he had done her, telling her of his deep sorrow, and of his determination in every way to atone for his evil deeds. His mother and Conrad joined their prayers to his; perhaps they feared that now she was surrounded by valiant and trusty friends Elizabeth would be revenged for all she had suffered, and would refuse to forgive them for the many and cruel wrongs they had inflicted upon her; they little knew the gentle, loving nature with which they had to deal. She spoke no word; she would not let it even seem as though she had anything to forgive, by pronouncing their pardon. She threw her arms round Henry's neck and mingled her tears with his; and the Duchess Sophia and Conrad joined in that kiss of peace, whilst the brave warriors, who had fought in the Crusades, could not restrain their tears as they saw the touching sight, and thought of the noble prince who was the common link between them all—who seemed to have spoken with loving voice, and bade them bury every wrong thought in his grave.

Soon all was settled; the duchies of Thuringia and of Hesse devolved by right upon little Hermann, but during his minority his uncle Henry was to be regent; Elizabeth and her children were to return to the Castle of Wartburg, where the Duchess was to rule, as she had ruled during the lifetime of her husband. And when the Crusading knights had thus accomplished their solemn vow they went to their separate homes, happy that God had allowed them to redress the wrongs of the widow and the fatherless, ready to serve their Landgrave's widow again, even to the death, should occasion offer.

All Germany had taken her part when her sufferings were known, and all Germany rejoiced with her when right was done, and Elizabeth once more reigned in her husband's castle.

CHAPTER XVI.—1228-1229.

Elizabeth's life at Wartburg — The world's censure — The Pope's
messages and letters cheer her in her trouble — Elizabeth's
longings for the religious life — S. Francis d'Assisi — The poor
Clares — Elizabeth appeals to Maître Conrad — He refuses to
grant her request — She asks her brother-in-law to assign her
another home — Her life at Marburg — Good Friday in the
Franciscan Chapel at Marburg — Elizabeth's triple vow — She
assumes the habit of the Franciscans — Her children leave her.

THE young Duke Henry nobly kept his word; by every
mark of affection and respect towards his sister-in-law
he sought to atone for all the injuries of the past, and
to show his penitence before God and man. But there
were others who even now wilfully misunderstood her,
who could not believe in the life of a saint, who would
not honour her because she was so immeasurably
superior to them.

To go back to Wartburg was to return to the old life
which she had led during Louis' absence from his
home; to visit the poor, to nurse the sick, to protect
the orphan, to bestow her alms freely, almost lavishly
upon all around her, was the one joy and comfort of
her lonely existence. She could do even more than in
former days, for her deep mourning was a sufficient
excuse for absenting herself from the festivities of the

Court, and in silence and solitude she sought to practise that voluntary poverty which she had ever held in such high honour. Such a life, however, did not fail to bring down censure upon it from those who could not enter into the pure and holy motives which prompted it. The rich and the great heaped insults upon her, because she despised those worldly things which were their chief delight; if they passed her when she was bound on some errand of charity they would remark, in a voice loud enough to be heard, that she was a *fool* and *mad.* And yet she was so patient and so joyous, there was such a sweet and heavenly calm upon her face that her enemies said she had already forgotten her husband, and had ceased to mourn him. Even the Duchess Sophia listened to these tales, and reproached her daughter-in-law with them; but this did not distress Elizabeth; she knew that God read all that was in her heart, and the peace and joy that reigned there were His own especial gifts, which the things of this world could neither give nor take away.

Morning and night she went forth upon her errands of mercy and of love, fearing no human censure, caring for no human praise, seeking only to be near Jesus in poverty, near Him in acts and deeds of love. And although worldly men scorned and despised her, there were those who looked on and wondered, and gave thanks for the bright light S. Elizabeth shed round

about her, and amid her troubles a glad softening ray
of comfort came to her from afar, and from a most
unexpected quarter.   The fame of her holy, self-
denying life, of trouble so meekly borne, and hardship
welcomed and hailed with joy for the sake of Christ,
reached the Pope, Gregory IX., at Rome, and he sent
her several messages, and addressed to her many
letters in which he assured her of his interest in her
welfare, and of his prayers for her, and he bade her
persevere in the life she was now leading, not fearing
the taunts of her enemies, but putting all her trust
first in God and then in him, for as long as he lived he
would stand her friend, and would never fail her.   He
gave her a church and cemetery for the new hospital of
S. Mary Magdalene, which she had begun building at
Gotha during her husband's lifetime, and the com-
pletion of which had been her first care and thought on
her return from her exile ; above all he ordered Maître
Conrad of Marburg to take more especial direction of
the soul which God destined for such high and holy
things, and to defend her to the full extent of his
power against the temptations that came to her from
without.   But gradually in these early days of her
widowhood there came into Elizabeth's mind an increased desire for the Religious Life, a wish to dedicate
herself altogether ; for the remainder of her days to
God, in the holy state of poverty.   Even now earthly
cares and troubles came between her and the Bride-

groom to whom she so longed to be united; earthly
love, her yearning tender affection for her little ones,
sometimes took her thoughts away from the sole contemplation of Jesus.

There was a long and bitter struggle ere she made
up her mind to leave all that was most precious to her
on earth, for we have seen how ardently and passion-
ately she could love; how her heart clung to those
friends and relations whom God had given her. All
through her life she had tried to let the things of
heaven take the first place in her heart; and those who
knew her best, who saw the holy, saintly, daily struggle,
the longings and strivings for perfection, would have
said that she had succeeded nobly—that there was
naught that she need give up. But she in her humility
and self-knowledge saw far otherwise; and so in those
peaceful months, when circumstances allowed her to
withdraw from the gaieties of the court, she sought for
strength to fulfil the purpose which she felt God had
put into her heart. She gleaned all the information
she could relative to the Religious Orders then existing
in the Church; and none seemed to her so likely to
satisfy her needs, to enable her to live that life of
voluntary poverty, which she had ever held in such
high veneration, as that Order founded by S. Francis of
Assisi, and to which she in some sense already belonged.
The three vital principles of the Franciscans were the
principles of all religious communities; poverty,

chastity, and obedience. But their poverty was not only the renunciation of all worldly possessions, but of all property, even in the clothes they wore, in the cord which girt them, even in their Breviaries. They were not to receive money in alms, except to aid a sick brother; they were literally to fulfil the precept, if smitten on one cheek to offer the other: if robbed of a part of their dress voluntary to give up the rest. Mutual love, of the deepest, holiest kind, was to be their bond of brotherhood; obedience was to spring from love. The Saint of Assisi had hesitated at first between the active and contemplative life—between constant prayer and praise in the seclusion of the monastery, or preaching the Cross of Christ to sinners. The mission of love was chosen; and the success of the Franciscans, the converts they made, the love and zeal they showed, never has been, never can again be equalled on earth.

There were women who listened to S. Francis' fervent eloquence, to his words of mystic, passionate tenderness, and who felt that they too, if they would be perfect, must lead the life of poverty, which he set before them as the highest and best life. Clara, a noble virgin of Assisi, had striven against all earthly love and affection, and had entered into a convent attached to the Church of S. Daman in her native city. She became the mother of the Sisterhood, which still numbers many a pious holy woman in the Roman

Church—that of the poor Clares. Their life was one
of entire poverty—of long, never-ending penance ; and
this Order it was that S. Elizabeth determined upon
joining with her director's approval.

She went one day to Maître Conrad and told him
all that was in her mind ; but he most indignantly
repudiated the idea, telling her that her sex and rank
rendered her totally unfit for such a life. She had so
set her heart upon it, so believed that she was acting
according to the will of God, that she would not
believe he was in earnest, and still persisted in her
entreaties, which he with equal obstinacy combated;
and at last she left him, weeping bitterly, and saying:
"You will see that I shall do something which you
cannot forbid."

It was a terrible disappointment to the ardent, loving
soul; a lesson in that obedience to which she wished
to give up her life. Such lessons come to many of us
every day; we long to do some great thing for God, to
show our love for Him by some great act of self-
sacrifice, and He bids us wait, and by waiting patiently,
show our sincerity;—" to obey is better than sacrifice."
He bids us gaze upon that life at Nazareth, that long,
long patient waiting of more than thirty years, when
the Saviour in His humble home saw sin and iniquity
rife in the world, and longed with all the love of His
Sacred Heart to do the work He had been sent to do—
to redeem those lost souls. But His hour had not yet

come; and so He waited on, an example to all those who are longing and yearning to do God's work. This hour will come to us all; perhaps to some of us it has come already, although not in the way we would have chosen. We *may* be doing, we *must* be doing His work, by our submission to that very authority which seems to hold us back from Him.

S. Elizabeth returned to her daily life and to the duties of her home, trying to learn the lesson of submission; but still although Maitre Conrad had forbidden her to enter the Religious Life, he could not prevent her living as nearly as she could to it in her own home.

So she asked her brother-in-law to assign her some residence where she could give up her life wholly to God, and where nothing could interfere with her works of piety and charity.

Henry, who although he could not understand his sister-in-law's goodness, and marvelled at it behind her back, was always gentle and respectful to her, he gave her the sole possession of the town of Marburg in Hesse, and bestowed upon her the sum of five hundred marks for the first expenses of her establishment. The young Duchess thanked her husband's family most warmly for their goodness to her, saying that it was much more than she either deserved or had expected. She left Wartburg with many tears, and journeyed to Marburg, where she appointed the officers

who were to rule her household, and won all hearts
by her loving gentleness.   Maître Conrad does not
seem to have approved of this change in the residence
of his spiritual daughter, for he wrote to the Pope that
it was not by his advice that the Duchess left
Thuringia to establish herself in his native country.
However he does not appear to have forbidden the
step, and himself accompanied Elizabeth to her new
home.

Whilst she was living her quiet life, and thinking
only how best she might serve God, her fame had
spread abroad throughout all Thuringia and Hesse,
and now the people of Marburg sought to do her
so much honour, and to show her how they had
felt for her many sufferings, that she was pained and
distressed by the homage she received, and she retired
to a little lonely village on the banks of the Lahn,
about three miles from the town, and there she took
up her abode in an old tumble-down hut; for she
would not be a burden upon any of the poor peasants,
who only longed for some opportunity of serving their
new mistress.   The roof of her new abode had in many
places fallen in, and her only shelter from the rain,
and the wind, and the sun, were the friendly branches
of some noble trees which overshadowed the cottage.
She prepared her own food, which was of the simplest,
coarsest kind, and she never sat down to a meal
without sharing it with some poor beggar, who had

L

wandered from Marburg to ask the charity of the noble lady, who seemed almost as poor as her guest.

In the meantime she ordered a small house to be built for her in Marburg, in which she might live among the poor people as one of themselves. It was constructed of wood and clay, just like the dwellings of the meanest of her subjects, that they might see that she had come amongst them, in all things to share their life and poverty.

To this poor home she brought her little children and her faithful servants; and there she led a life strict, rigorous, self-denying as even the Poor Clares themselves within the walls of their Convent at Assisi. Still there was the earnest, irrepressible longing to give herself up to God, by some irrevocable vow, to be acknowledged by the world as belonging to Him, so that none should ever again associate her name with earthly love or earthly greatness.

We have already seen that some time, before her husband's death, she had become a penitent of the Third Order of S. Francis, but she was bound by no vows, she was only associated with the Franciscans by mutual prayer and deeds of love; this was all that was required of those persons who longed for a holier life, and still were unable to give up the world altogether. Now, she wished to make a public profession of her attachment to the Order; to take before the Church, that vow of poverty, chastity, and obedience, which already she had taken before God. She wished to give to the Franciscans herself, and all her worldly possessions; all that she had was to belong to the poor.

Maître Conrad approved of her design; and in after days this Third Order of S. Francis assumed the character of an entirely Monastic Order, taking S. Elizabeth as their patroness.

When all was settled, when she had received permission to do in this matter all that she thought right, she spent her time in yet closer acts of prayer, in still more ascetic practices; for she knew that she still had much to give up—much that was most dear to leave behind her, ere by her own act she dedicated herself entirely to God. "I know," she said, "that I need three great gifts from my Lord and Saviour. Firstly, a complete contempt for all earthly things; secondly, courage to despise the injuries and calumnies of men; thirdly, and this is the hardest of all, to give up the affection I bear my children." It was for these gifts and graces she prayed, and fasted, and strove so earnestly; and at last one day she went to seek her companions, and a light was upon her face, which had nothing of earth about it, and her voice trembled with exceeding joy as she said: "The Lord has heard my prayer; all the riches and pleasures of the world, which once I valued so highly, are now as nothing to me. As to the calumnies of men, the stories invented by the wicked, the contempt I inspire, I feel proud to suffer them all. And my beloved little children whom I loved so well, whom I embraced with such loving tenderness, well even these are as strangers to me now, I call God to witness it. I offer and confide them to Him, that He may do with them as He wills. I no longer love anything; I no longer love any creature; I only love my Creator."

And now Elizabeth longed only to take the vows which she felt would be to her such sweet and joyous servitude. "If I could," she said, "find a habit coarser and poorer than that of the poor Clares, I should adopt it, to console myself in some measure for not joining that sacred Order; but, alas, I cannot hear of such an one." These events happened during Lent; Passion-Tide had dawned upon the earth, telling its mingled tale of agony and of love; and now Good Friday had come, that day when the Church tells her children of that steep ascent up Calvary's hill, when the Lord of Glory fell three times beneath the weight of the cruel Cross, when we listen to those last words of Him Who hung there all those long hours for our sakes, and which He left as a most precious legacy to the faithful for evermore; when the cry of human agony issued from the Sacred Lips of the God-Man, and then all was over, and the world was redeemed from the curse of sin. On that day, in the Franciscan Chapel at Marburg, the kneeling crowds, who had come to adore their Lord in the Most Sacred Mystery of the

Passion, looked upon a sight such as they had never seen before, but which was in strange keeping with the hour, when Jesus, robbed of even the very clothes He had worn, hung naked for us upon the Cross. In memory of this no ornament was upon the Altar; no holy Sacrifice was offered on that one day in all the Church's year. Elizabeth's children were there, and many of her friends, and numbers of Franciscans, and she herself knelt before the Most Holy Place; and there, in the presence of those she most loved on earth, she broke the last links which bound her to the world, and gave up all, to follow the Heavenly Bridegroom Who had called her to Himself. The threefold vow was taken; Elizabeth of her own free will gave up her friends, her children, her all, that she might serve God alone. Her beautiful hair, which fell in massive raven tresses almost to her feet, was cut off, and she was clothed in the coarse grey habit and the girdle of cord, which were the distinctive marks of the Order of S. Francis.

To the day of her death she wore that sacred garment; and, in addition to the rules of the community, she always voluntarily went bare-footed; she, the royal lady, was the most humble of them all. Guta, her faithful maid of honour, who had been her most trusted friend from her infancy, would not be separated from her beloved mistress now in the new and higher life upon which she had entered. On that

same Good Friday, when Elizabeth bade adieu for ever
to all worldly things, the young girl took the habit of
the Third Order of S. Francis, and renewed the vow
of chastity, which she had taken long before.

There was one more trial yet to undergo ere the
loving heart of Elizabeth could be at rest. The
children whom she loved so tenderly must be taken
away from her. Months ago the thing would have
seemed to her impossible, now, she saw the loving
Hand of Jesus, pierced with cruel nails, stretched
out to welcome her ; she heard a Voice more gentle
and tender than the voice even of her dead husband
or her little children, saying in softest, gentlest accents,
" Every one that hath forsaken houses, or brethren,
or sisters, or father, or mother, or wife, or children,
or lands, for My sake, shall receive an hundred-fold,
and shall inherit Everlasting Life."

She took her darlings one by one into her arms,
and blessed them with choicest blessings, and prayed
for them with words of burning love ; then without
a sigh she let them go, for she knew God would be
ever with them.

The little Duke Hermann, his father's heir, who
was now six years old, was taken to the Castle of
Creuzburg, there to be safely watched and cared for,
until he should be old enough to hold the reins of
government which his uncle now held for him. His
eldest sister Sophia accompanied her brother to his

new home; the little girl was already affianced to
the young Duke of Brabant; Elizabeth's second
daughter, who was also named Sophia, went back to
the Abbey of Kitzingen, which was her home to the
end of her life, and where she took the veil; the
little two-years-old Gertrude, her mother's especial
darling, was sent to a convent at Altenberg, near
Wetzear. It was a poor place enough, of but recent
foundation, and every one marvelled that Elizabeth
should choose such a house for the training of her
precious child. Some even went so far as to
remonstrate with her upon the subject; but she gently
replied that all had been settled between herself and
her husband on that last day when they had bade each
other farewell for ever, before the child was born.
"Heaven inspired us to choose this convent," she said,
"for God wishes my daughter to help to advance
the spiritual and temporal welfare of this holy house."

In after years the Saint's prophecy was abundantly
fulfilled, for the young Gertrude became Abbess of
Altenberg at the age of one and twenty years, and
the fame of her pious life went abroad into all nations.
Now all was over, the sacrifice accomplished, the
yearning desire of a whole lifetime fulfilled at last.
The world sneered and wondered, and pitied the
mistaking zeal which had induced a princess of
royal birth to give up all the vain pomp and glory
of the world, all that was most precious to her on

earth, for Christ's sake; they held that such conduct
was unnecessary, wrong, unworthy of her duties as a
mother; that her proper place was with her children,
doing her duty in that state of life in which God
had placed her. So the world argued then, so there
are many who at the distance of more than six
centuries will argue now. And truly it would not
do, if all acted as S. Elizabeth did. But there are
souls to whom God has spoken in all ages, souls to
whom He speaks now in a peculiar and special manner.
There are some whom He bids remain in the world,
doing the work He has set them to do, serving Him
well and rightly in the way which He has appointed
for them. There are others whom He calls nearer
to Himself even on earth, whom He bids enter the
solemn cloister, and live a life of poverty, and pray
for those who dwell in the busy haunts of men.
And generally He calls those with His own gentle
voice who have the greatest capacity for loving, whose
hearts are bound to those whom He has given them
to love. It was so with S. Elizabeth: we have seen
it in her passionate affection for her husband, in
her tender devotion to her children. And He Who
hallows every human tie, hallowed this; but He is
a jealous God, and He wanted the heart that could
love so well, to love Him alone. And so step by
step He called the Duchess of Thuringia to Himself;
He made her understand that He would' watch over

her little ones, but that the care of them came between her and her religion, and she must needs give them up. And she obeyed and triumphed at last, and the loving gentle woman became one of God's own chosen saints.

CHAPTER XVII.—1229.

ELIZABETH was alone now with her maids of honour in the hut which she had had built in Marburg; she had given her life to God, as we have seen, for many years; but worldly cares and worldly affections had taken up some part of her time, she was for the first time free to devote herself, and all that she had, to the service of her Lord and Master.

She considered nothing her own, and although Maître Conrad had forbidden her to make a formal renunciation of her property to the Church, she gave away all that she had; she never spent one penny of it upon herself, indeed her care now was to seek some means of gaining her own living. She took to spinning wool for the Religious, of the Convent of Altenberg. They sent her the wool, and when she had spun it she sent it back to them, and they paid her for her labour.

Sometimes they were not over-exact in their accounts; she on the contrary was ever most scrupulous in her money transactions, and one day when she had been paid beforehand for some work, and was unable to finish it because she was obliged to undertake a ourney to Eisenach with Maître Conrad, she sent back the piece of wool that was left, together with the money, which she felt she had not earned.

In these days she suffered from extreme weakness and illness; all the hardships of the past were telling upon her now, whilst her hard ascetic life must have been singularly trying to a constitution which was not naturally a strong one, and which had been impaired by the agony of mind she had endured when her cruel enemies chased her from her husband's home.

Often she was obliged, although much against her will, to spend the whole day in bed, but even then she insisted upon going on with her work; and when at last her companions took away her spinning wheel by gentle force, she would not remain idle, but prepared the wool for another occasion.

Out of her humble earnings she always deducted some offering for the Church; with the rest she purchased the coarse food for her little household, sometimes indulging the others in a somewhat more luxurious repast, but never herself deviating from the rule she had laid down as the one she must ever pursue. The good people in the town would sometimes

bring her some savoury little dish they had prepared
for her with their own hands. She would smile and
thank them so warmly that the poor things went
away quite happy, believing that for once " the dear
Elizabeth " would have a good meal. But as soon as
they had taken their departure, the Duchess ran off to
her hospital, and stood over some poor sick creature
doing ample justice to the good cheer which had been
so carefully prepared to please her royal palate. In
fact she would have fasted with rigorous discipline,
had not the doctors told her that such a course
would be her death; and so with her usual obedience
she yielded to their wishes, only taking care that
the food necessary for her, should be of the commonest
kind.

She loved to perform the most menial offices ; not
that she might obtain the praise of men, but that she
might humble herself before God, and show Him that
she was indeed the poorest and meanest of His
creatures. And yet whilst she worked as a common
servant, her soul was ever engaged in prayer and
contemplation, and often whilst she was standing
before the fire cooking the simple dinner for herself
and her attendants, she would become so absorbed in
holy things, that she often, all unconsciously, allowed
the coals to fall upon her dress and burn great holes
in it ; nor was she in the least aware of what had
happened, until her companions came in choked by

the smell of the burning wool, of which she, rapt in meditation, had been utterly unmindful.

An old writer gives a somewhat quaint description of S. Elizabeth's attire, which from poverty seems to have assumed something of the grotesque. The grey habit was much worn out, and as it does not seem to have entered the Duchess's mind to procure a new one, she tried to remedy the evil by patching it here and there with pieces of different coloured cloths; she insisted upon doing this herself, and as she was anything but a skilful workwoman, in fact knew nothing at all about the management of her needle, the effect of the many colours filling up the holes which had been produced by rents or burning was somewhat peculiar. Her cloak, which was of the same material as her dress, had shrunk with the frequent exposure to rain, and in order to lengthen it she added on a piece of a totally different colour. She seemed to see nothing peculiar in all this; her extreme simplicity and total self-forgetfulness had always been her great charm, and continued to be so to the end; men might laugh and jeer at her if they pleased; once she had cared for such things; now they had no power to hurt her. Sometimes, too, she gave away one or other of her coarse garments to some poor, half-clad beggar whom she met in the streets of Marburg; and when the winter was at its coldest, she would sit shivering near her little fire, or get upon her bed and lie between two mattresses, saying, with something of the old child-like joyousness, "Here I am lying as if in my shroud."

Amid all this simplicity of living the Duchess was as gracious and affable to all as when she ruled within the walls of her husband's castle. No tale of woe was ever carried to her, but that she listened to it with tender sympathy, giving what help she could, always sending those who sought her advice from her presence with a feeling of thankfulness in their hearts that they had been to her ; if it had done nothing more for them, it had shown them the exceeding beauty of a saint-like soul, and for that they thanked God, whilst they called down many blessings upon S. Elizabeth's head.

To those immediately about her she was always most kind and courteous; she would allow them to give her no title of worldly honour; she bade them call her by her simple name of Elizabeth—the name God had given her when He made her His own child in Holy Baptism. She also insisted that they should use the more familiar pronoun *thee* and *thou* in addressing her, in preference to the formal you, which was generally accorded to her. She made them sit beside her at meals, herself often taking the lowest place.

Nothing ever seemed to irritate or put her out; no hardship or discomfort ever called forth one word of discontent from her lips—to bear was her duty; to bear cheerfully was to bear for Jesus' sake, to be near

Him in privation and suffering. She loved to talk to her companions of the goodness of God; she was always bright and joyous, as those must be who always realize His ever-abiding presence, but anything like levity pained her more than all else; she would rebuke the offender very sweetly, but very firmly, saying: " Where is the Lord now ?"

The care of the sick had always been her especial delight, as we have seen in the days when she lived in the world; now she devoted herself to them more than ever; nursing them, feeding them, speaking to them of the health of their souls, whilst she tried with her own sweet gentleness, to soothe and allay their bodily pains. She had built a hospital at Marburg, which she had dedicated to the blessed memory of S. Francis d'Assisi. The blameless and gentle Saint had died in 1226, and had just been canonized by Gregory IX. The Pontiff thought that the royal lady, who sought in all things to follow the bright example of the Saint, was worthy of receiving some more precious gift than that old cloak which he (as Cardinal Ugolino) had persuaded S. Francis to send her. In the solitude of Monte Alverno the Saint of Assisi had retired to hold a solemn fast in honour of S. Michael the Archangel. Thrice the Scriptures had opened before him as he knelt at the part of the Holy Gospel which records the Passion of our Lord; and then S. Francis saw in a vision, a seraph with six wings; amidst these wings appeared the likeness of the Crucified. And as the vision disappeared there came upon the body of S. Francis marks of the Crucifixion like those which he had seen. There were the five wounds of the Redeemer imprinted on the person of his Saint; from his side, blood would frequently flow in crimson streams. All this he sought in his humility to hide from his disciples; but at last it was discovered, and Gregory IX. judged that the most precious present he could send Elizabeth would be some of those drops of blood which had flown from S. Francis' side when he received the Divine *Stigmata.* He could have sent nothing that she would have valued more; the most costly gift could not have equalled this in her eyes; for it seemed a new link to him who appeared in his life of poverty most closely to have followed the despised Nazarene.

The sacred relic was placed with all reverence in the hospital; and there day after day Elizabeth spent her time amongst her rich and her poor. She had, as we have seen, performed degrading offices in her hospitals at Eisenach, but those that now came into her daily life were more revolting to her nature than any she had yet undertaken; she dressed the most loathsome wounds, she gazed upon the most painful sights; and although her tender heart bled with exceeding pity, and her whole nature sickened at what she had undertaken, she went through it all bravely and unflinchingly; it was but another way she knew of breaking her own will—of subduing the love of ease and luxury and refinement, which she always said clung to her with such strange pertinacity in spite of all her efforts to the contrary. It was the last method she employed of conquering the flesh, of loving what was most repugnant to her, because each poor diseased body contained a living soul, and for that soul "Jesus, her Love, was crucified." In each poor suffering creature she saw the Divine Spouse of her heart, Who left to those who would work for Him amongst His poor His own Divine promise: "Inasmuch as ye have done it unto one of the least of My brethren, ye have done it unto Me."

The world wondered at what they saw, there were even pious souls who said that the Duchess went too far, that such intense self-devotion could not be right. Too far. Ay, yes, surely it was so, if indeed we *can* go too far, if we *can* do too much for Him Who died for us. If we can limit what we owe Him, then we can afford to condemn those who have served Him as S. Elizabeth did.

One day the Duchess met a poor beggar in the streets, as she was wending her way to church; she turned back at once, and took him to her hut, and washed his hands and feet, and bade him welcome here. But somehow on that particular day she recoiled from her task, and a shudder passed through

M

her as she pursued it. She was angry with herself
for the feeling, and scolded herself thus : " What poor
unfortunate, does this disgust you ? know that it is a
most wholesome drink ;" and as she said the words,
she drank some of the water she was using, saying :
" O My Lord, when Thou wast stretched upon Thy
Holy Cross, Thou didst willingly drink vinegar and
myrrh, I am not worthy of such a drink, help me to
become more worthy."

In past days, too, we have seen her special devotion
to lepers : to those poor outcasts of society whom the
Lord Jesus had healed from all their sins ; now she
again tended them with special care, washing and
clothing them, and taking them to her own poor home,
and honouring them as though they had been of equal
rank with herself. "Oh, how happy we are," she
would sometimes exclaim, " thus to be able to clothe
and to wash our dear Lord."

But her zeal had reached such a pitch, her self-
abnegation had become so entire, that Maître Conrad
felt his duty to interfere, and to bid her cease from
those holy practices which were at once her pleasure
and delight. He bade her not touch or kiss these poor
leprous creatures, for by so doing she ran the risk of
infection. She obeyed him, as she ever did ; but she
felt the deprivation so keenly, it was so hard to her
to give up that loving impetuosity which was a second
nature to her, that she became for a time seriously ill.

Although she was forbidden to do as she had done before, although she was obliged to put some restraint upon her works of love, she was allowed to labour as much as she pleased for the salvation of the poor, erring creatures whom God sent to her day by day. All her care was to let them receive the Sacraments of the Church, and hear of pardon and of peace from God's own Priests. Sometimes they would not listen to her; they had wandered too long in the ways of sin to hope for mercy now; and they turned a deaf ear to the gentle voice which pleaded with them so lovingly. But with all her meekness Elizabeth was very brave in her Christian zeal; and she went on in the strength of her right purpose, putting before those hopeless, despairing souls the love and Mercy of Jesus; and at last she triumphed, and weary ones found rest in the Holy Sacraments of God's own appointment. On one occasion as she stood with Maître Conrad at the door of the hospital a blind man craved admittance; she willingly granted it, and begged him at once to seek help for his soul in the Sacrament of Penance. He laughed her to scorn, telling her "that such things were idle superstitions in which he did not believe." She was very indignant as she listened to his words of blasphemy, and for an instant she spoke sharply, forgetting His blessed Example, "Who, when He was reviled, reviled not again." Then she remembered the sin of which she had been guilty; even for His dear sake she felt she must not be angry; and so in all humility she knelt at Maitre Conrad's feet, confessed her fault, and asked for pardon. The old chroniclers do not tell us the sequel of the story; but surely we may hope that the blind man was won over by that sight of submission and humility.

It was not only in her hospital that she appeared as a ministering angel; in the streets and lanes of Marburg, wherever sickness or sorrow were to be found, there Elizabeth was ever seen, giving them all the help she could; if she had no money, distributing amongst them the jewels she had worn in the short bright days of her married life.

Once a sick person who had eaten nothing for many days fancied some fish—there was none to be found in the town; it was the depth of winter, and no one went fishing in the Lahn in such inclement weather, particularly as they were almost certain that they should catch nothing. Elizabeth was sadly distressed at not being able to gratify her patient's whim; then suddenly she ran to a neighbouring fountain, and knelt down on the cold ground, and said, "Oh Lord Jesus Christ, if it be Thy will, give me some fish for Thy poor sick man." She let down the bucket to draw some water, and when she drew it up again a large fish was there, which she took with great joy to her patient.

But now once again Maitre Conrad remonstrated with her, because she took the poor people whom she

met in the street, and whom she considered worthy of
receiving her charity, to eat at her own table, sitting
down by her side as though they had been her equals in
rank. This time, however, she seems to have combated
his arguments, and to have been allowed for a time at
least to act as she pleased. " Oh, my dear master,"
she said, " let me have them ; think of my old life
spent in the pride and vain-glory of the world, evil
must be overcome by the practice of the contrary
virtue ; I must now live with the poor and humble,
such society bestows numberless graces upon me ; let
me enjoy it."

Again, however, Maître Conrad felt that he must
curtail what it seems he had begun to consider the
superabundant zeal and charity of his spiritual
daughter. There was a poor leprous boy who was
deserted by all his friends, who had lost his father and
mother, and who had no one in all the wide world to
care for him, or to speak one word of kindness to him
amid all his suffering. Elizabeth found him out, took
him home with her, dressed his wounds, nursed him
tenderly as his own mother would have done, ay
perhaps more tenderly, for in those days we read of
mothers deserting the children upon whom God had
set His mark of suffering. She spent many hours
a day beside his couch, soothing his sufferings, speaking
to him of that other life where there would be no more
pain. And she loved the poor fellow with the love of

that large heart of hers, which took in all who were poor and afflicted for Jesus' sake. Suddenly Maître Conrad hearing of all this, sent the poor child away, lest S. Elizabeth by her loving care might catch the loathsome disease.

But even now her boundless charity was not to be restrained. She found another poor boy, suffering from a malady almost as grievous as leprosy, and she took him home with her, and tended him lovingly with a skill which could only be learned in the school of religion and charity, of which Christ Himself was the Master. Fearful as this new patient's malady was, it was not considered infectious, and so Elizabeth was allowed to keep him with her until her death. He was one of the few allowed to be with her in the last hours of her life. Still poor lepers remained the objects of her most tender compassion, she even envied them their sufferings, because more than anything else, those sufferings detached the poor victims from all worldly things. One day when brother Gerard, the Superior General of the Franciscans in Germany, called to see the Duchess of Thuringia, she said to him with the tears in her eyes: " Oh, my father, I wish from the bottom of my heart that I might be in all things treated as a common leper; I wish that I could live as they live in a way-side hut, with a heap of straw for my bed, and a linen sheet hung before the door, to warn the passers-

by that it is a leper's home; and a box placed there
to receive their alms." When she had thus spoken
she fell into a trance, and the brother heard her
sing a sweet glad hymn, which told of the love and
the praise of Jesus.

In all ages of the Church we hear of the tender
sympathy and loving care which the saints always
bestowed upon those creatures whom God had visited
with the terrible scourge of leprosy. We cannot
wonder at it, for it was in the house of Simon the
eper that S. Mary Magdalene washed her Master's
feet with her tears; it was the leper Lazarus, whose
soul Jesus tells us of, partaking of the joys of Paradise.
And in the guise of one of these poor outcasts the
Lord came to His people to plead their charity and to
test their faith. In the early Church we hear of S.
Martin, the Apostle of Gaul, giving up his time to
comfort these afflicted beings, and healing them often
by God's mercy. In England, in the twelfth century,
the holy Bishop of Lincoln, S. Hugh, admitted the
lepers to Mass and to the kiss of peace. S. Louis of
France ever treated them with marked respect, whilst
in mediæval days S. Catherine of Sienna, S. Francis of
Assisi, S. Clare of Assisi, S. Edmund of Canterbury,
and many others, thought that the highest service they
could render to God was to tend upon and care for
those whom all else on earth shunned and avoided.
Centuries later, one who in many respects followed in

the footsteps of S. Elizabeth of Hungary, who like her was robbed of an earthly love, and sought her sole comfort in the love of God and in works of charity, S. Jane Frances de Chantal gave up her life specially to try and soothe those human pains which were hardest of all to bear, and which had to be borne all alone.

And now they wait—that blessed and glorious company, who on earth followed the Footsteps of their Lord, and whose lives were one long act of prayer and of self-sacrifice—yes, they wait for a little while in peace and joy beneath the golden Altar, until the Master's Voice bids them take their place at His Right Hand in glory everlasting. For the short life of earthly trouble and self-mortification has bought for them the life of never-ending, unceasing joys, and the love that was given up for Jesus' sake on earth is restored to them in full and most abundant measure in the Court of the Saints who dwell in the Heavenly Jerusalem.

CHAPTER XVIII.—1229-1230.

The King of Hungary hears of the strange life his daughter is
leading, and sends an Ambassador to Thuringia — Elizabeth's
reception of her father's friend — Her message to the King of
Hungary — She bestows her fortune upon the poor — The story
of Hildegonde — Elizabeth rejoices with those that rejoice.

JUST as, during her husband's lifetime, tidings had
reached the King of Hungary of the strange way in
which his royal daughter lived, and he had sent his
ambassadors to ascertain the truth of these reports,
so now again he heard from the pilgrims who returned
to his dominions from Aix la Chapelle and the Rhine,
of those seeming eccentricities of which all the people
of Germany were talking, which some praised and
some blamed, according to the light which God had
given them, to enable them to discern His own work
amongst them.

One thing, however, seemed to be quite certain: the
royal widow was living in a poor hut in a state of utter
poverty; and when the King heard this he shed tears
of bitter grief, and determined to send one of his
ambassadors into Hesse, to bring his daughter back to
her native land.   Probably he thought that she was
reduced to this dire strait by some new wiles of her

enemies, and determined at once to take her under his
all-powerful protection.

Count Banfi, the Hungarian messenger, was sent in
the first instance to Wartburg, to demand of the young
Duke Henry some explanation of the strange tales
which had reached the ears of his sovereign.

Henry answered that his sister had gone quite mad;
that every one knew it; and he begged the Nobleman to
go and see her, and to judge for himself of the utter
impossibility of reasoning with her. He gave a vivid
description of her life of poverty, and told all that he
had done for her, adding that riches were of no use to
her; that she cared for them only to bestow them with
lavish hand upon every beggar who asked her charity.
The Count, wondering at all he heard, proceeded to
Marburg. Having arrived there, he asked a publican,
at whose house he alighted, to tell him something of
the strange life led by Elizabeth, the young Duchess
of Thuringia.

Those who saw the daily life of this Saint of God,
who witnessed her many works of charity, who came
in contact with such gentleness and humility as they
had never before seen, could not but speak well of her,
if they told the truth; and so this poor man told the
Hungarian ambassador of the holy life the King's
daughter led in the town of Marburg; how day by day
the people thanked God for having sent her amongst
them, for she was more like an angel in their midst

than a human being; how they felt that it was for their souls' good that she had come there; and how they all loved the merciful, gentle lady, who was more humble than the poorest beggar in the place. After he had thus spoken in her praise, he conducted the Count to her poor house, opening the door, and saying in loud tones, " Madame, I think your friends have come to take you away; in any case here is one who wishes to speak to you."

Elizabeth was sitting at her spinning-wheel when her father's messenger appeared before her.

He was so struck with the strange sight, his master's daughter clad in that poor coarse garb, and working for her daily bread, that he made the sign of the Cross, and then burst into tears. " Was ever the like of this seen," he exclaimed, " a king's daughter spinning wool?"

Elizabeth welcomed him warmly, and asked him many questions about her father, and her dear old home; and when he had answered them, he told her that he had come to take her back to Hungary, where she would be loved and honoured by all.

" What do you take me for," she said; " I am but a poor sinner, who have never obeyed God's law I as ought to have done."

" Why do I find you in this miserable condition?" asked the Count, " who has dared to reduce you to it?"

" No one," was the gentle answer, " unless it be

the infinitely rich Son of my Heavenly Father, Who has taught me to despise riches, and to cherish poverty above all the kingdoms of this earth."

Then she told him the one object of her life; she tried to make him understand that solemn vow by which she had bound herself to God for ever. He would not understand her, he could not believe that any one could be so wilfully blind to their own worldly interests; he entreated her, " to return with him to her own country, to receive her own rightful kingdom."

She smiled as he spoke thus: " I hope, she replied, that I already possess, the inheritance of My Father, through the Eternal Mercy of our dear Lord Jesus Christ." When the ambassador saw that nothing would induce her to leave the country so dear to her, because it had been her husband's, he entreated her for her father's sake, to give up her present way of living, and to keep up some establishment more worthy of her royal birth and her high dignity.

She saw that he could not understand her; that he could not enter into the depths of that spiritual life which came before all else with her; so she gave him one last message for her father, and then he went away grieved to the heart at the failure of his mission, leaving her at her spinning-wheel to lead that life of poverty which she had voluntarily chosen; the king-doms of this world were as dross in her eyes, the love of Christ was her all; for having seen Him, she had loved Him and believed in Him, and preferred Him before all else. The good old King of Hungary, the descendant of a long line of saints, knew perhaps better than any one else, all that was in his daughter's heart, and treasured up those words which she had bade the Count say to him from her, and looked forward to meeting the child he loved so well in the life of the world to come, for Elizabeth had said: "Tell my father that I am more happy in this life, which men despise, than he can be in all his royal pomp; and that instead of fretting about me, he ought to rejoice that he has a child given to the service of the King of heaven and earth. I ask but one thing of him in this world, that is to pray for me himself, and to ask others to pray for me, and I will pray for him as long as I live."

This visit of her father's ambassador to her humble home was the last effort ever made by Elizabeth's friends to draw her back again into that world which she had renounced; they saw that her resolve was taken, that she had given herself wholly to God, and that nothing would ever make her see things as they wished her to see them. So she went on living at Marburg, leading the life that to her with all its hardships was a life of exceeding happiness; able to minister to the wants of others out of the dowry which her brother-in-law, in spite of his opinion that she had

gone mad, most scrupulously paid her. Perhaps he
was afraid of the Pope who had constituted himself the
young Duchess's protector, and so did not dare go back
from his plighted word, or perhaps Conrad of Marburg's
all-powerful influence was exerted here, as it was in
many other quarters. However it may have been,
Elizabeth's dowry was always at the service of her poor
neighbours, whilst she worked and spun for her daily
bread. The riches that God had given her were indeed
laid up as treasure in heaven, to be given back to her
as lent unto the Lord after many days. She sold all
her jewels, even the vases of gold and silver which she
had brought from Hungary as her marriage portion;
then when she received from the Duke the five hundred
marks which he had promised her, to defray the
expenses of her new household, she determined upon
distributing the money amongst all the poor within
seventy-five miles of Marburg, and she issued a proclamation ordering them all to appear before her on a
given day, and that they should then receive what she
considered their due. On a great plain near Wherda
a strange company assembled in obedience to the
Duchess's command. Crowds of beggars were there;
the lame, the blind, the sick, and infirm, young and
old, all anxious, eager, and excited, jostling against
each other in their haste to reach the place where their
benefactress stood. She, however, had given orders
that those who pushed before their companions were to

be punished, and the punishment was to consist in having their hair closely cropped upon the spot. One young girl, whose name was Hildegonde, left her place in the ranks, and hurried away to seek her sick sister. It was instantly thought by the officers whose duty it was to see that the people remained where they had been stationed, that she was one of the culprits, that she had already received her share of the money, and was trying to obtain a double portion by joining one of the other ranks. On this supposition all her beautiful hair, which had been her chief adornment, was cut off, and she was led tearful and ashamed into the presence of Elizabeth. Something in the fair young face attracted the notice of the saint; she seemed to read there that Hildegonde's hopes and aspirations soared above the things of earth, that in spite of her grief at the loss of her hair, the seeds of a higher and better life were in the girl's heart. She asked her if this was not the case, if she had never thought of living for something more than the things of this world; and Hildegonde answered with downcast eyes that she would long ago have taken the habit of a Religious, but that she could not bear to part with all her beautiful hair.

When the Duchess heard this she joyfully exclaimed: "I am happier because they have cut off your hair, than I should have been, had my son been elected Emperor of Rome." She took the poor girl home with her, and she worked in Elizabeth's hospital, and consecrated herself to God in the service of His sick and poor.

The whole of that vast multitude assembled on the plain of Wherda received Elizabeth's bounty; she passing between the ranks and giving them the money with her own hands, whilst a quiet happiness was on her lovely face, upon which sorrow and suffering had left something of its impress; she was so thankful to be able to do something for God's poor, so grateful to Him Who gave her this great pleasure of lightening some of the sorrows and troubles which He sends to the sons of men. "The king's daughter," as has been rightly said, "was indeed in the only court which pleased her; really a Queen on that day by right of her exceeding mercy, whilst her subjects were the poor, and weary, and suffering ones of the earth." And to those upon whom she so graciously bestowed her alms she appeared to be something more than human, even her poor clothes had received some strange new lustre, they were white as snow as she moved amongst that suffering band, whilst upon her face there shone a light as though Angels had touched it with their wings, and left something of their radiance there.

Night came on; the bright moon rose in all its splendour, shining upon the faces of those whom Elizabeth had made so happy on that day. Bands of poor creatures, talking gladly of all they should do now that they had a little money, prepared to return to their cabins, some of which were of course at a great distance off; there were others already tired with their long journey, who could not think of returning home that night, and who sought the best shelter they could find in Marburg, many of them finding a night's lodging beneath the hospital walls and the adjacent buildings. Elizabeth looked out and saw the poor things doing the best they could for themselves; her tender heart was moved with pity for them; she would willingly have opened her own doors to receive them, but her little hut was hardly large enough for herself and her attendants; so she went out amongst the people and distributed more alms, and with her own hands gave each of them a good supper. Then she caused large fires to be lighted, and round these, motley groups assembled, old men and women bowed down with age and infirmity, and quaint little German children with their yellow hair and bright blue eyes, revelling in the unwonted good cheer. In their joy and gratitude they began to shout and sing, and make merry; and when Elizabeth heard them a deep feeling of joy and gratitude was in her heart, and she went out amongst them once more and took part in their happiness. Her own sorrows had not made her forgetful of the Apostolic command, "to rejoice with those that rejoice, as well as to weep with those

N

that weep.   "To make all around her as bright and cheerful as possible, was one of the duties she imposed upon herself; one of the few earthly joys of that brave, unselfish nature was to cast some gladness into the lives of others.   And as those poor people sat in the bright light of the moon that night, and the flickering shadows of the fires fell upon their worn, pinched faces, lit up with the strange new happiness of being thought of and cared for; perhaps amongst them all, there was no heart so light as her's who had given them all this pleasure, for " it is better to give than to receive."

CHAPTER XIX.—1230.

Maître Conrad of Marburg seeks to break Elizabeth's will by forbidding her to bestow her liberal alms — The tradition of how she sought to evade his orders — Maître Conrad's excessive severity — The visit of Rudolph of Varilla to Marburg — Elizabeth's patience and thankfulness under calumny — Her faithful friends are sent away from her by her Director — Those who replaced them — Elizabeth gives up her children for ever.

THE chequered, troubled life of which we have been writing is now drawing to a close, the trials of earth, the self-imposed discipline, the intense asceticism have fitted the soul for the Master's garden, and from afar " faint fragments of the song " seem to be falling upon the ears of her who so longed to be with Christ. But there was still greater discipline to be endured ere the end came, more entire submission of the will before the work was done, and the rest Elizabeth so yearned for, was obtained.

There were many amongst the faithful in those days who judged that the means which were used to break that humble child-like will, were unreasonable and unjustifiable; upon this we need not enter; we are not writing the life of Maître Conrad of Marburg, so we shall simply state facts as they occurred, without

N 2

either condemning them or justifying them. That Maître Conrad was a faithful servant of God and a devout son of the Church none can doubt, but that his zeal sometimes carried him beyond the limits of discretion must be allowed. On that very occasion when he took the poor leprous boy out of Elizabeth's loving care, he gave her so severe a penance that he afterwards himself asked a penance from the Pope for his rashness. In training S. Elizabeth, he felt he was training a Saint for God, and so if he strove to break her will in every way, to render her entirely obedient in everything, we can but believe that he was acting as he thought best for the glory of God, and we know that the Lord allowed His Saint to bear these new and heavy trials which were imposed upon her by his Priest. In the early ages of the Church we read similar acts of seeming tyranny which all redounded to the praise of God, and to the eternal happiness of his Saints; and if what was her greatest earthly joy and consolation was taken from Elizabeth by order of her Confessor, although that joy was derived from obeying God's own command, and giving up all that she had to His poor, still the blessing of obedience brought with it its own reward, and again we say: "to obey is better than sacrifice." God does not bid each of us give up the same thing; what is a penance to one may be pleasure to another; all of us must relinquish what costs us something. He asks at our hands that in which we most delight, holy and pure and good though that pleasure may be. And so we shall see how through his Priest He bade Elizabeth resign the one joy of her life. There seemed nothing else of which he could deprive her, her husband was dead, her children were far away, banished from her by her own free will·; she had renounced all the pomps and vanities of the world, there was not a single comfort or luxury of which she could be robbed, but there was the (to her intense) luxury of giving away ; of keeping nothing for herself but of bestowing all she could upon others ; and now this was to be taken from her, her alms-giving was to cease. Maître Conrad forbade her not to bestow more than one single farthing upon the poor, only a denier, the ancient and lowest copper coinage of the country, was to be given to the poor beggars, who so humbly craved the charity which had never yet been denied them.

There is a tradition of those times, however, (which seems to receive some confirmation, from the fact that some small silver coins called *Elizabethan Pfennige* are still to be found in many Museums,) which narrates that Elizabeth tried to disobey what seemed to her so impossible a command, by causing some deniers to be struck, not in copper but in silver, and so satisfying her conscience by giving a coin which was

really worth a *schelling* of the coinage of the realm.
And when the poor people who were accustomed
to her generous gifts received so little and appeared
astounded and dissatisfied by her seeming parsimony,
she said: " I am forbidden to give you more than
a *denier* at a time, but I am not restricted to giving
it you only once." They were not slow to take
advantage of the permission ; so they would go
away for a little time and then come back again,
numberless times during the day. Maître Conrad
heard of the innocent ruse employed by Elizabeth
in order to obey him, and yet to help her poor people,
and instead of being touched at the boundless godlike
charity which would not be repelled, he was very angry,
and is even said to have struck the Duchess several
hard blows as a punishment for what he chose
to term her disobedience.

She bore it patiently, she almost rejoiced at it,
for she thought of One Who had never sinned and yet
Who meekly stood and was scourged and buffeted
by his enemies ; and must not she who sinned every
day of her life, take this little chastisement from him
who, hard although he appeared to be, laboured
only for the good of her soul ?

Still Maître Conrad determined to achieve what he
had begun ; and he now strictly forbade his spiritual
daughter to give away any money under any form or
pretext whatever, allowing her still, however, to dis-

tribute bread to the people as she had been wont to
do.   After a time he took this last pleasure from her,
telling her that she must not give alms of any kind ;
she was only to show her love to God by nursing the
sick and infirm ; lepers—those for whom she felt such
especial tenderness—were not to be tended by her
she must give them up into the care of others.   Once,
and once only, she saw some poor, suffering creature
who sorely needed her help, and unmindful of Maître
Conrad's prohibition, she did what was needful for the
leper ; her punishment was a severe beating, which she
bore with her usual gentleness.

Her grief was very bitter when little by little all
that she had delighted in doing for God's poor was
taken from her ; we can imagine what it was to her to
meet those who had lived upon her bounty, and whom
she was now forbidden to help : truly it was the
greatest act of self-abnegation, the most entire subjec-
tion of her own will that could have been imposed
upon her ; how hard, how difficult to endure, we leave
those to imagine whose greatest pleasure is to
give to others.   And yet no impatient word ever
escaped her lips ; the only thing that made her angry
was when any one in her presence laid any blame upon
Maître Conrad for his treatment of her, for she had
begun to see that although she had seemingly given up
all she had to God, she had kept one thing back, and
that was her *will ;* now that must be offered Him, bent,

broken, worthless, except that He might order it as He would. It was the final triumph of her life of self-abnegation; it was the victory which must be learned by all those who would be taught by Christ. It was the end and rule of those three and thirty years of that most perfect Life, beginning with the first cry of the Holy Child in the Manger at Bethlehem, ending with the cry when all was indeed "finished" on the dark Mount of Calvary.

In all things small as well as great the Duchess of Thuringia sought to obey the somewhat despotic commands of her director. She owned she was afraid of him, but only as God's minister acting thus towards her. "If I thus fear a mortal man," she said to her attendants, "how should I not tremble before God, Who is the Lord and Judge of all men." She had given her own will into the hands of Conrad, because he had abjured all thought of earthly greatness and advancement, and like herself had chosen the life of poverty.

Her gentle obedience to all his commands did not, however, seem to win the stern Priest to greater indulgence towards her; on the contrary, day after day he demanded fresh sacrifices from her; he even occasionally placed her into temptation solely that he might chastise her. On one occasion he sent for her to come to him at the Convent of Altenberg, where her little daughter Gertrude lived. The nuns, hearing of her arrival, asked Maître Conrad to allow her to enter the cloister, so that they might see her of whom they had heard such wonderful things. Now the rule of the Convent was that no one was to be allowed to intrude upon the privacy of the nuns under the pain of severe punishment. He had told Elizabeth this; but when she heard him in answer to the nuns' solicitations say, " Let her go in if she will," she took it as a permission to enter. Conrad soon made her come away, and then he showed her the book in which was written the oath by which she had promised to obey him in all things, and he ordered a monk to beat her and her attendant Irmengarde with a large stick which stood near ; and whilst his stern order was obeyed he chanted the *Miserere.* She bore this as she had borne all else ; and afterwards in talking it over with Irmengarde, whom she had so unwittingly drawn into the same mistake as herself, she said: " We must patiently endure such chastisements, for we are as reeds which grow on the river's bank ; when the river rises the reeds bend, and the waters flow over them without breaking them ; afterwards they right themselves, and rise in all their strength and rejoice in new life. We also must sometimes be bent to earth and humiliated, and afterwards we rise with joy and confidence."

Again, one day Conrad was preaching a sermon on the Passion of our Blessed Lord, which he was particularly anxious that Elizabeth should hear, but she was occupied with the care of some sick people, and did not appear. When the sermon was over he sent for her, and asked the reason of her absence, and before she could answer he gave her a violent blow, saying, "That is to teach you to come next time when I expect you." Once more, with a sweet smile upon her face, Elizabeth sought to excuse herself for her seeming disobedience; but again Maître Conrad struck her, and this time so severely that the blood began to flow. Then the gentle Princess raised her eyes to heaven, and said, "Lord, I thank Thee that thou hast chosen me for this." Her women gathered round her in terror, and when they saw that her clothes were stained with blood, they asked her how she could have submitted to such harsh treatment. Again she smiled and answered, "So that I may bear it with patience, the good God has allowed me to see Christ among His angels, for Maître Conrad's blows sent me up to the third heaven." When these words were repeated to the Confessor he exclaimed, "I shall always repent that I did not send her up to the ninth heaven."

It seemed now as if Elizabeth's cup of bitterness was full, as if no fresh trial from without could come into the sad young life of three-and-twenty years; and yet one more was in store for her, one harder, more startling and bitter than any she had yet endured. There were those in the world still who would talk evil of her; they had called her a fool and mad, now not knowing what to say they laid a still more grievous charge at her door, and accused her of a great sin. The story of Maître Conrad's chastisements had gone forth exaggerated and embellished, for people in the thirteenth century discussed their neighbours, and threw stones at them, just as people in this nineteenth century do, and they said that there was too much familiarity between Elizabeth and her director, that the intimacy between them was not what it ought to be. The base, groundless rumour reached the Court of Thuringia, and Rudolph of Varilla, the Duchess's tried and faithful friend, went to Marburg, and gently and respectfully as he could told her what he had heard. She did not answer him; perhaps even now she dared not trust herself to speak, lest the foul calumny should betray her into saying some word of which she might afterwards have repented. She raised her eyes meekly to heaven, and fell upon her knees, and said, " O Lord Jesus Christ, I bless Thee and thank Thee that Thou hast deigned to receive this poor offering at my hands; for the sake of Thy love, and to be as a servant in Thine eyes, I have given up my noble birth, my rich possessions; I have tarnished my beauty and my youth; I have renounced my father, my country, my children, all the consolations of life; I have made myself a beggar; I kept back but one thing, my honour and my reputation. But Thou askest this of me also, I give it Thee with all my heart, as Thou deignest to accept as an especial

sacrifice my good name, and makest me pleasing in
Thy sight by ignominy. I consent to live as a dishonoured woman, but oh, my Saviour, preserve my
little innocent children from any shame that may fall
upon them on my account."

Then she showed her old friend, so as to assure him
of her innocence, the marks upon her shoulders, caused
by Maître Conrad's hard blows, and she told him that
such was the love by which the Priest was animated,
or rather by which he sought to make her love God.
Rudolph of Varilla saw and wondered, and was con-
vinced of Elizabeth's innocence, and went home to
Thuringia to tell of the saintly life of obedience which
Louis' widow led in her poor home. Amid all the
sorrows that had come into Elizabeth's existence there
had been one bright, ever-present ray of human
comfort. Her two faithful maids of honour, Ysentrude
and Guta, who had known her as a happy child, as a
somewhat sorrowful maiden, and then as a loved and
honoured wife, had been one with her in all things,
since that cold winter's day when the inhospitable
gates of the Castle of Wartburg were closed against
the young widow and her little helpless children.
Their loving care had been her only solace in all the
sad weary time that followed; they had stood with her
by the side of her husband's coffin, and every work of
charity, every deed of love had been shared by them
and cheered by their gentle sympathy. Their life, like

hers, was given up to religion; she felt that in loving them she was not loving the world, and the thought of separation from them never once entered her head; their affection had lightened her many burdens, cheered her many sorrows, helped her through many a difficulty. There were other faithful attendants who had followed her into her life of voluntary poverty, who one by one had been dismissed by Conrad, and whom she had seen depart with keen regret; but these two were left her; Ysentrude and Guta must surely be with her to the end, which something now told her was not very far off. But Conrad feared that their society might cause her to look back upon her past life, sometimes to talk of its splendours and then to regret them. It was hardly likely that this would be the case, but the implacable director argued otherwise. He sent away Ysentrude first, the one whom Elizabeth loved most dearly, from whom she had never hidden one single secret either of joy or sorrow. Ysentrude herself thus writes of that bitter parting: "I was sent away, I Ysentrude, whom she loved better than all the others, and she parted from me with heart-broken agony and with countless tears." Then it was Guta's turn to go; Guta, who had never left her royal mistress since she was five years old, was now wrenched from those loving arms and carried away, leaving Elizabeth alone to sorrow for her loved companions until the day of her death. Her

solitude was of short duration; all she craved
was to be left with God, she wanted no human care,
no human sympathy. But this Conrad would not
allow, he replaced her two faithful friends by two
other attendants very different to those he had
taken from her. One was a peasant girl, also named
Elizabeth, coarse, rude, and so horribly ugly that
she frightened all the children who came in her way.
The other was an old widow, deaf and soured, who
spent all her days and nights getting into violent
passions.

For the dear love of Christ, Elizabeth bore with
these two, asking God to help her, and to make her
humble with the coarse, rude peasant girl, and patient
and gentle with the old passionate widow. It was a
hard task, for both women seemed in league to humi-
liate her in every possible way; they left her all the
coarse work of the house to do; they ordered her to
cook the dinner, and upbraided her when it was not
done to their taste; they delighted in acting as spies
upon her, and telling Maître Conrad whenever they
had found her, moved by some irrepressible feeling of
compassion, bestowing her own poor meal upon others.
Nothing, however, seemed able to vex the saintly lady
who was so hardly used by him to whom she felt
bound by a solemn and irreparable vow of obedience.
She would never willingly transgress his slightest
command; and when sometimes her dear old friends

came to visit her, she would offer them no food because she could not do so—could bestow nothing on another without her director's express permission.

It seems as though up to this period Elizabeth had sometimes allowed herself the pleasure of having one of her little ones with her for a time ; and those were sunny days in her life when her children sat upon her knee, and she talked to them of God and of Jesus, and of their brave father who had died in that far-off land on his way to fight for Christ. Now, however, her darlings were to be banished from her for ever. Perhaps she felt that the sight of them drew her heart from God ; that she must not run the risk of letting those so infinitely dear come between her, and the Holy Bridegroom of her heart ; perhaps Maître Conrad ordered her to forego what might be a temptation to her ardent, loving, clinging nature ; be it as it may, now, when Ysentrude and Guta had been taken from her, her children also were sent away for ever.

CHAPTER XX.—1231.

Mediæval miracles — The deaf and dumb boy is cured — The blind
man receives his sight — The doubts that came into Elizabeth's
mind — Her life of prayer and meditation — S. Elizabeth's
Well — Her devotion to the Saints — Her ideas on the subject
of Church ornaments — The treachery of the beggar she had
sheltered — The visit of the Angel — Perfect peace comes into
the troubled life.

THERE are many who will receive the story of Elizabeth's patient sufferings with something of incredulity,
who will turn away perhaps with something of unbelief
from the record of those miracles, which in the last
year of her life it was granted her to perform, and
which we shall notice very briefly. But before we tell
the tale of those wonders which God allowed His Saint
to set forth before the world, ere He took her to Himself, we will quote the words of one whose name is
held in highest honour amongst us, (Dr. John Mason
Neale), and see what he says of the faithlessness which
rejects the miracles wrought by the servants of God in
these ages of the Church, which men falsely called
"the dark ages." "To disbelieve Mediæval Miracles
is to reject Mediæval history; for whether we excuse
our incredulity by asserting that the biographers of

saints fabricated their actions, or were so grossly credulous as to attribute not once only, but thousands and thousands of times, supernatural agency to everyday occurrences; whether in short we impugn their veracity or deny their common sense, we equally affect their credit as historians. It may be, indeed, very possible that in several instances phenomena, explicable to us by our superior knowledge of second causes, may be attributed by them to the direct interference of the First; but in myriads of cases a miracle cannot be denied but by the supposition of an intentional falsehood. And whether then is it more likely that the laws of Nature should have been, in confirmation of our Saviour's promise, suspended at the prayer of faith, or that men famous in the Church should have lied to the Holy Ghost, Whose assistance they often begin by invoking? . . . . . . Now as a matter of fact mediæval miracles are generally and most unhappily disbelieved amongst us. To dwell upon them would depreciate instead of adding to the reputation of the saint of whom they were related; we must argue not from Mediæval Miracles to Mediæval Holiness, but from Mediæval Holiness to Mediæval Miracles. A miserable thing that we should have to argue the subject at all! A heartless consideration that works written in the spirit, in which we endeavour to write, must so soon become valueless, as saying either too much or too little! Till better days come we would

o

earnestly pray that the eyes of both those for whom we write, and of all others, may be opened to see the majesty and the loveliness of the Mediæval Church; so to see it as to endeavour, each for himself as far as may be, to restore it."

But a very few, then, of the miracles which it was granted to S. Elizabeth to perform shall be written here in all faith, to be received as God shall point out, to those who read this simple chronicle of a holy life.

One day as the Duchess of Thuringia, in her simple coarse dress, was passing through the streets of Marburg, on her way to the hospital, she saw a poor boy stretched before a door-way, his limbs so fearfully contorted that he was only able to walk on his hands and knees; the poor child was, in addition to his other infirmities, deaf and dumb, and his mother had left him there helpless and alone, in the fond hope that Elizabeth would pass by and would have pity on him. She was not mistaken; the kindness and charity that never failed were brought into action now; the Duchess bent tenderly over the poor afflicted boy, and asked him where his parents were, and how he came to be there? There was no answer, and Elizabeth looked into the pale, sad face, and saw the story of the child's great affliction written there. "In the Name of Jesus Christ," she said, "I command you to tell me from whence you come, and who brought you here."

The boy answered simply : " My mother brought me here," and then he told her how all through his life he had never spoken, never walked ; now one by one his limbs were straightened and he thanked God for the cure which he had wrought by the prayers of S. Elizabeth ; she in her humility mingled her thanksgivings with those of the happy child, and bade him go home and tell his parents what God had done for him, but she forbade him to mention her name, only she told him ever to remember her in his prayers, as she would ever remember him. But when the boy reached his poor home and his parents heard him speak and saw him walk as others did, they asked him who had done such great things for him ; and he answered " A sweet lady in a grey dress ordered me to speak in the name of Jesus Christ, and instantly my mouth was opened." The mother knew who it was that had done this for her son, and perceived Elizabeth taking flight in the distance. In her great joy and thankfulness she spread abroad the wonderful miracle, and there were others in that poor cottage who every day of their lives prayed for the " good lady in the grey dress."

Another day she was alone in the little chapel of the hospital which she had built. It was mid-day, and every one had gone home to dinner, only a poor blind man groped about helplessly, and the Duchess seeing he was seeking some one, went up

and asked him what he wanted there. He told
her that he was seeking the dear lady who was
so good to all the poor, intending to ask an alms
of her, but he had first come to say a prayer in the
church. He recounted to her all the sad story of
his life, how he had never seen God's own bright sun,
how he had never been able to work for himself but had
always been poor and wretched and miserable. She
tried to comfort him by telling him that his sad
affliction had saved him from many a sin into which
he might have been drawn had he had the gift of sight,
she made him see that God had sent him this trial
for his own good ; but he answered that he would have
kept out of sin, that he would have worked hard
and honestly for his own living ; and she, moved with
compassion, said : " Pray God to restore you your
sight, and I will pray with you." As she said these
words the blind man guessed who it was that was
speaking to him, and he fell down at Elizabeth's
feet and begged her to have pity on him ; but again
she only bade him pray fervently, and she knelt and
added her supplications to his, and even as she
knelt God granted to the blind man the precious
gift of sight. He thanked her for her great goodness,
but she disclaimed all merit, she told him to show
his gratitude by avoiding sin, by working as an
honest man, and being humble and loyal in all he
undertook.

Countless more miracles might be recorded, but these are enough to show how God showed to the world before He took her away from it for ever, the exceeding saintliness of her who like her Divine Master had been despised and rejected of men. It was not only to the bodies of the servants of God that she showed all her love; it was not only human ills she prayed might be conquered. There were those whose minds were darkened to all the truths of the Christian faith, whose friends sought her pious intercessions, and light dawned upon the souls that never before had known the love of Jesus.

But even now, when God allowed the faith of His servant to triumph so signally, her old humility never deserted her, indeed sometimes she was the victim of doubt and self-reproach; she did not seem to love Him enough Who did so much for her. Amid all the brightness of her spiritual life there were hours of darkness to be endured, at which she shrank and trembled. Such temptations and doubts come to all the servants of God Who seek to serve Him as they ought, for there were three hours' darkness ere the Lord's own Voice spoke and told that the work of Redemption was done.

Elizabeth united in a wonderful manner the active and the contemplative life; all day like Martha she served her Lord in labours of charity, and when night came, unmindful of fatigue, she would kneel

at His Feet for hours, praying for His Grace and
Mercy, and meditating upon His Life and Death
of love. Sometimes she would leave the Church,
where crowds flocked to see the Saint whose fame had
pread abroad in the world, and in some lonely fields,
and beneath the canopy of heaven, she would kneel
and pray to the Creator of the world. An old tradition
relates that one day, as she was thus praying, the rain
poured down in torrents, soaking all around; she alone
escaped being wet. There is a little fountain, which
is called to this day " S. Elizabeth's Well," which is
situated in the midst of a lonely wood, at the foot of
a steep mountain about six miles from the town
of Marburg; and there more than six hundred years
ago the Duchess of Thuringia retired day after day,
and wept, and fasted, and prayed. A steep and
dangerous path led to this favourite resort of her's,
and a tiny chapel was built by her orders near the
well, where she could worship God without fear of
interruption. Every Sacrament and Rite of the
Church was treasured by her beyond all else; she loved
to dwell upon the lives of the Saints, and to seek to
imitate their bright example. Next to her own patron
Saint, S. John the Evangelist, all her devotion was
given to S. Mary Magdalene; those two held the
dearest place in her heart, second only to the Most
Holy Trinity and to the Ever Virgin Mother of God.

She prized ornaments as accessories to devotion, but

none knew better than herself how to render them no higher place than that which faith and love assigns to them. On one occasion she visited a monastery, and the monks assembled around her, and pointed out to her the excessive beauty of the sculptures which adorned their church; she turned to them very gently, and said in her own sweet way: "Truly the money you have spent on this would have been better employed in clothing and feeding you, for you ought to have all this sculpture engraved upon your hearts." She rigidly practised the severity in these matters which she preached to others; once she was entreated to buy a statue of marvellous beauty, and she answered, "I do not need the image: I carry it already in my heart." And the image of God was indeed impressed upon the soul of His chosen Saint. Time passed on, the goal was nearly reached, and her life shone out with still more beauty—even the cloudless serene beauty of a summer's day, which seems more glorious and perfect ere it sinks to its rest. One morning a poor woman to whom to whom she had given a night's shelter suddenly disappeared, carrying with her all her benefactress' coarse garments. Elizabeth, having literally nothing to wear, was obliged to remain in bed. " My God, I thank Thee," she exclaimed, " that Thou hast made me like unto Thyself; for Thou camest naked into the world, and Thou hangedst naked upon the Cross." Even as she spoke an Angel appeared to her, as he had done in bygone days when she gave her mantle to the poor beggar on the mountain of Wartburg, and he said to her: "I do not bring you a Crown now, as I did before, for God Himself will soon crown you with His Glory."

And so in sweet communing with God, and with His holy Angels, the last days of that life of four and twenty years passed quickly away; following in the blessed track of "the Disciple of Love," it seemed as though some faint, far away Vision of the bright glory of the Heavenly City was granted to her "who loved so much."

No sorrow had power to touch her now; no sign of trouble was ever to be seen on her face. That sacred gift of tears which God had bestowed upon her, and which we have already noticed in her early life, was her's still; she cried very much in those last days of her pilgrimage, wept perhaps for the wickedness which she saw around her. But these copious tears left no mark or disfigurement upon her fair face; did not disturb the calm serenity of her lustrous eyes. Those tears told what she could not find words to say; in the joy that came with the thought of death, she could find no other means of thanking God for all the mercies that had followed her through her life.

CHAPTER XXI.—1231.

Elizabeth's vision — Her great joy — Her preparations for her happy journey — The last days and hours of the saintly life — Her last wishes — The last Sacraments — The death of infinite peace — The Office of the Dead — The flight of the birds — The sorrow shown by all — The burial — The Canonisation of S. Elizabeth — The translation of her remains — The scene in the church at Marburg.

It was the year 1231. Already S. Anthony of Padua the loved disciple of S. Francis d'Assisi had been called to his rest and to his sure reward, and now another saint was to swell the army of Paradise and to bloom in the garden of the Lord. S. Elizabeth's course was wellnigh run, light, sure light was coming at eventide after the short and troubled days. She who had despised the kingdoms of this earth, was to dwell with the Angels now. Yes she was to rest from her labours, but in all ages of the Church her works would follow her.

One night as she lay half asleep, half praying, for even in her sleep she seemed to pray,—a bright light shone around her and a sweet voice, which was the Voice of the Lord, said: " Come Elizabeth my bride, my friend, my beloved, come with Me to the house

I have prepared for you from all eternity ; I will take you there." When she awoke she knew that her summons to the Home for which she so pined had come at last ; she made all the necessary arrangements for her happy journey, she gave all directions relative to her burial; she went to see her sick and her poor for the last time. Maître Conrad was just then very seriously ill, and he sent for his beloved daughter to visit him in what he believed to be his last hours. True to her mission of consolation she hurried to him and was received by him with all love and honour and respect ; but he was very anxious to know what she would do when he should . have left her, to what spiritual director she would 'go, who she would trust to guide and advise her as he had done. She could not but smile in her exceeding joy and happiness as she answered : " Your question is a useless one ; I shall die before you, I shall never need another director."

Four days more passed away, and she watched and prayed, and waited for the promised deliverance ; then a strange lassitude came over her, her head and limbs ached, and her skin burned like a coal of fire ; she could not rise from her bed, she knew that she should never again get up ; but that that illness would be the last bodily pain she should ever feel. For a fortnight the fever lasted, but Elizabeth was always bright and joyous, always praying that she might bear her sufferings patiently, even to the end. One day when she seemed to be sleeping, her face turned towards the wall, her attendant heard a sweet melody, which seemed to fill the room ; and then the Duchess turned round and said, "Where art thou, my beloved?" "Here I am," replied the girl; "but oh, Madame, how beautifully you were singing just now." "What!" said Elizabeth; "then you too heard something; I will tell you what it was. A beautiful little bird came and perched between me and the wainscot, and he sang to me so long and so sweetly, that my whole heart and soul rejoiced, and I felt obliged to sing also."

"Doubtless," remarks an ancient writer, "the Saint's Guardian Angel took the form of a little bird, and sang to her of those eternal joys to which she was hastening."

She felt that the end was very near now; and in order to prepare for it, she bade farewell to all her acquaintances and friends, blessing them, and telling them that the short remainder of her time must be given to God; that no earthly thought must distract her from the contemplation of the Day of Judgment and the great Judge of the world. So they all went away from her sobbing bitterly, and left her with her attendants, her Confessor, and the little boy who had taken the leper's place in her love and care. With many tears and prayers she besought the Mercy of God; and on the Eve of the Octave of S. Martin

(November 13th, 1231,) after Matins, she made her last confession to Maître Conrad, who had sufficiently recovered his strength to be at her bedside, and who listened now with tearful eyes, as she laid bare her whole soul before him, and asked for absolution for her many sins. But every fault had long ago been bitterly mourned for, and washed away by the most sincere contrition. Her confession ended, and the grace of pardon through the Precious Blood granted to the dying Saint; Conrad asked her wishes as to the bestowing of her worldly goods. "I am astonished" she answered "that you should ask me such a question, for you know that since I took the vow of obedience I renounced all that belonged to me, at the same time that I gave up my will, my children, all my mortal pleasures; I have kept nothing but what was absolutely necessary in order to pay my debts and to give alms, with your permission I had long ago given up all, and lived in a little cell, receiving my daily bread with the poorest and most despised of earth. For a long time all that I have seemed to possess has really belonged to the poor, give them all I leave, only keep this old habit and let me be buried in it. I make no will; I have no other heir than Jesus Christ." But one of her companions asking her to bequeath to her some especial legacy, she gave her the precious cloak which S. Francis d'Assisi had sent her all those years ago. "Do not mind its being all torn and mended and miserable; it is the most precious of my earthly possessions. I declare to you that every time I have wanted some special grace from God, I have gone and prayed to Him covered with this mantle and He has answered my desires." She asked to be buried in the chapel of her own Hospital, but she said nothing more then about her funeral; she was thinking too much of her entrance into Paradise.

Mass was said by Maître Conrad, and as the hour of Prime drew near, the last Sacraments were brought her: that Precious Food for which she longed, which alone would strengthen her soul for its passage through the dark valley of the shadow of death. When she had received Extreme Unction, then communicated (for in that age of the Church Extreme Unction always preceeded the Sacred Viaticum), she lay quite still and calm for the remainder of the day; meditating upon that Blessed Sacrament, which to her was a pledge and a foretaste of the joys of the Land of Rest. Generally she had been somewhat reserved on the subject of religion; it was seen in her daily life more than by the words she spoke: her excessive humility often kept her silent when others discoursed of the things pertaining to the Kingdom of God. Now on that last day of her mortal race her tongue was suddenly loosed, she seemed to remember all the sermons she had ever heard, all the good

books she had ever read, and she spoke of them in
burning, eloquent words to her attendants as she lay
there with the shadow of death upon her face. She
repeated all the Holy Gospel that tells of the raising
of Lazarus from the dead, and dwelt with especial
delight upon that gracious condescension of Jesus in
visiting Mary and Martha, and consoling their bitter
grief, mingling His Divine Tears with their human
sorrow. Then she spoke of those Sacred Tears of
Jesus, and her words were so wonderful and beautiful,
that those about her wept as they listened to her, and
though that soon indeed they should hear her and see
her no more. She saw their grief, and spoke the
words of her Lord as He walked to His Death up the
steep ascent of Calvary: "Daughters of Jerusalem,
weep not for Me, but weep for yourselves." Even in
that last hour she thought more of others than of
herself, seeking to console those who sorrowed so
bitterly because she was going to leave them. Then a
sweet and delicious harmony filled the humble little
room, and when her attendants wondered from whence
it came, she said: "Did you not hear those who sang
with me? The music was so beautiful, that I was
obliged to join in it as best I could." The echoes of
the angelic song, that for so long had sounded in her
ears, were truly very near now; already the bright
celestial beings were carolling their glad welcome to
the dying Saint. The whole of the evening of that

never-to-be-forgotten day Elizabeth remained in that happy, joyous state which we have described; and when midnight came she turned to her friends, and said: "What should we do if our enemy the devil appeared to us now?" An instant afterwards her voice sounded strong and clear through the little room: "Away, away, wicked one! I have denied thee." It was the last of earth's temptations overcome by the victory of faith. Soon she spoke again: "Now he is gone, let us speak of God and of His dear Son Jesus Christ; do not let me tire you, my friends, my beloved ones, it will be but for a little time." Her face shone with so holy a light that those around her could scarcely bear to look at her. Then again, as midnight sounded from the old church tower of Marburg, she cried: "This is the hour when the Blessed Virgin gave to the world the Holy Child Jesus, the Saviour of men. This is the hour when Jesus became Incarnate, when He lay in the humble manger, and when a new star, such as had never before been seen, was brought to light. This is the hour in which He came to redeem the world, and He will also redeem me. This is the hour when He raised the dead, and when He freed the souls that were chained down by sin; He will free mine also from the chains of this miserable world."

Each moment her weakness increased and so also did her joy. "Yes," she said, "I am weak but I suffer no pain, I do not feel ill. . . . I commend you all to God." Still she lay on as though in a sweet and blessed dream, ejaculating from time to time fervent prayers and aspirations to God. At last she exclaimed, " Oh, Mary, come and help me ! for the time has come when God calls His friends to the marriage. The bridegroom has come to seek His bride." Another pause, broken only by the tears and sobs of those who gazed upon the marvellous sight, and heard the words of exceeding love poured forth from the depths of Elizabeth's soul. Once more she spoke : " Silence—Silence," was all she said ; she could bear no sound of earth to interrupt the glad melody of the heavenly song, which even then sounded in her ears. Meekly she bowed her head ; just as all through her life she had bowed to all God sent her, so now with that last outward sign of humble submission she breathed her last, she received her order of release from all earth's sorrows and trials. In the dark November night (it was the 19th day of the month), she went to where light perpetual would shine upon her for evermore. The poor little hut was filled with a sweet fragrant odour, and those who wept and prayed beside the dead heard the sound of clear voices singing that beautiful response which the Church puts into the mouths of those who like S. Elizabeth of Hungary, have given up their lives to God. *Regnum mundi contempti propter amorum, Domini mei Jesu Christi, quem vide, quem*

amavi, in quem credidi quem dilexi. The kingdom of
the world and all its glory I have despised for the love
of our Lord Jesus Christ, Whom I have seen, Whom
I have loved, in Whom I have believed, and Whom
I have preferred."

They did her bidding, those sorrowing friends whom
she had left on earth to mourn her for a while;
they washed the precious body with loving care, and
they laid her in her old grey habit as she had desired
they should. Ysentrude and Guta were there; and
the coarse country girl, and that cross old widow
who had replaced them as her attendants, and whom
she had won over at last by her sweetness and gentleness, mingled their bitter tears with those of her
tried and faithful friends. Then the Franciscan
brothers carried her body to the little humble chapel
of the hospital of S. Francis, where her days and
nights had been spent in prayer, where she had
struggled for strength to give up all to God; where
she had made the sacrifice of her will to Christ, and
won her great and glorious triumph.

Crowds followed her body to its last resting place;
and the tears and lamentations of the poor, her own
especial friends, almost drowned the funeral chants
which were sung by the Priests as they walked in
solemn procession from the little hut which had
been the Saint's home, to the hospital where she
had comforted and soothed many a poor sufferer.

P

For four days the corpse was exposed to view, whilst the poor, the sick, all who had loved her so well, crowded round the coffin to take one last look upon that face which had never worn anything but smiles for them, and which was more beautiful in death than it had ever been in life. For of late years there had been marks of sorrow and suffering upon the young and lovely features; now the roundness of youth had come back again, death had lifted whole years of grief from Elizabeth's fair brow. The calm majestic loveliness had never been surpassed in the days when her beauty was at its zenith. Happiness too was written there, where before there had been deep lines of care; and those who looked upon the dead Saint knew that for her life had indeed begun. On the fourth day she was laid in her quiet grave beneath a humble stone in the hospital chapel. And the grief of the mourning crowds broke out afresh when they felt that she was for ever hidden from their sight. Comfort only came when they thought of her exceeding joy, and remembered how as she had ever prayed for them on earth, she would pray for them still in the Paradise of the Saints.

The night before her funeral, whilst the Priests were singing the office for the dead, an Abbess who had come from a distance to take part in the solemn rites of the Church, heard without, the most exquisite melody that had ever yet fallen upon her ears. She went accompanied by several other persons to see what it could possibly be ; and on the roof of the church they saw a flight of birds, of a kind hitherto unknown, filling the cold wintry air with their sweet glad melody, as though they too would take their part in the funeral of the Saint. Writing on this subject, S. Bonaventura says : " These little birds bore witness to her purity by speaking their language to her at her burial, and in thus singing so sweetly over her tomb. He Who once rebuked the folly of the prophet by the mouth of an ass, might well proclaim the innocence of a Saint by the music of these sweet birds."

Very soon her simple tomb in the hospital chapel became the scene of many a miracle, of many a prayer answered, of many a vow taken in all faith and humility, by the simple German people who flocked thither to ask the prayers of the Saint.

Five years afterwards there was a noble and goodly company gathered in the little Town of Marburg, where Elizabeth had spent her life of poverty. Ever since her death Maître Conrad had employed his time in endeavouring to procure his dearly loved daughter's canonisation. None knew as he did how she merited it ; none but himself could have told all that sad and glorious tale of her spiritual life. Ere he could accomplish his purpose he died a cruel death, and another Conrad, Elizabeth's own brother-in-law, besought the Pope no longer to delay proclaiming

P 2

to the world the sanctity of the young Duchess of Thuringia. Gregory IX. yielded to the wish of the faithful, and on Whitsun Day in the year 1235 in the little town of Perugia, where S. Francis d'Assisi seven years before had been canonized, his saintlike companion's name was inscribed in the Kalendar of the Catholic Church. It was a well deserved honour, a public recognition of the virtues of her whom the world had condemned and censured whilst she lived, and whose prayers they now asked. But long ere the Pope's Bull went forth to the nations of the earth, S. Elizabeth's name had been written in the book of life, S. Elizabeth's voice had joined in the prayers of the saints. It was one year after this that that goodly company to which we have alluded was assembled in Marburg to do honour to the Saint. The Emperor Frederick II., who at last had been reconciled to the Pope, found his way to the humble Hessian town. From all nations pilgrims flocked to the tomb of the king of Hungary's daughter. It is said that twelve hundred thousand Christians inundated the town of Marburg on that memorable 1st of May 1236, when the remains of Elizabeth were to be translated, and laid in the rich and costly shrine prepared for them. The Duchess Sophia and her sons, and the four little children who were so honoured as to call the Saint, Mother, had come to take part in the ceremony. On the

morning of the appointed day, the Emperor passed
through the kneeling crowds who thronged the entrance
to the chapel, and with great difficulty was enabled
to penetrate into the interior of the building. He
walked bare-footed, he was clad in a coarse grey
garment, his only ornament was the Imperial Crown
upon his head; the princes of the empire in their rich
robes of state were with him, and in royal procession
they advanced to the tomb of her who had been the
most humble of the daughters of earth. The sacred
relics were exposed to view; they were still entire; no
trace of corruption was to be found there, after all
those years of interment. A sweet fragrance still
breathed around the tomb of the gentle lady who on
earth had shed abroad the gracious odour of her works
and deeds of love. Frederick placed a golden crown
upon the Saint's head, saying, in a voice choked with
emotion: "As I could not crown her whilst she lived
as my empress, I wish at least to crown her to-day as
an Immortal Queen in the Kingdom of Heaven." He
then led the young Landgrave Hermann to make his
offering at his mother's tomb, and his empress
(Isabella of England) in like manner led the little
Princesses by the hand. The Duchess Sophia and her
sons then went forward and did honour to the Saint;
once they had wronged her cruelly, to the end perhaps
they had doubted and misunderstood her; now, full
justice was done her; honoured for evermore in the

Catholic Church would be the name of "the dear Elizabeth."

Now in Marburg we find her still honoured, brought as it were daily before the minds of those who have wandered from the faith of their fathers, and who condemn the doctrine and truths which were so dear to S. Elizabeth. Still she seems to speak to them as they walk along the great streets of the picturesque little town which contains S. Elizabeth's Gate, S. Elizabeth's Well, S. Elizabeth's Bridge, S. Elizabeth's Mill, and above all there is the church, the first stone of which was laid by Duke Conrad in 1235, some months after her canonisation, which is dedicated to her honour, and rears its stately spire above the clear bright waters of the Lahn, standing in a garden of roses, which here as elsewhere seem to be the flowers specially associated with S. Elizabeth. More than forty years elapsed before the beautiful church was completed, and now in it purity and simplicity it is considered the most perfect specimen of Gothic architecture in Southern Germany. But the interior of the noble edifice has for three centuries been sorely neglected. The altars have been robbed of their beauty, and Lutheran hands have defaced much that Catholic piety raised to the honour and glory of God, and in loving memory of S. Elizabeth. The story of the short life of mingled joy and sorrow stands out in bas-relief upon the walls; sadly mutilated are the sculptures now, but there is depicted the scene on the mountain side when Louis discovered the beautiful roses in his young wife's mantle; there is the parting between the husband and wife; her deathbed, and that solemn scene in the little hospital-chapel when the Emperor laid the golden crown upon her brow; and the stranger is shown the silver urn which enclosed the sacred relics, until one of her descendants in his Protestant zeal scattered them to the winds. Perhaps brighter days are in store for the Church of S. Elizabeth's adopted country; perhaps the stones which lead to her tomb in the chapel where it was placed, and which are worn with the footprints of the many pilgrims who sought comfort there, may once again be trodden by those who reverence and love the one Catholic and Apostolic Church which S. Elizabeth would have given her life to save from false doctrine and heresy.

Strange indeed does it seem that three centuries after her death the Castle of the Wartburg, which had been the bright home of her happy married life, was tenanted by none other than Martin Luther, who sought shelter there from his enemies. And now tourists visiting the place gaze at the stains on the walls made by the reformer's ink as he wrote those heretical doctrines which were to go forth to the world, and carry foul poison with them; and as they look at the likeness which hangs there and depicts the burly form and coarse features of the heretic, they forget that bright pure presence which once reigned in Wartburg; they ignore the memory of the Saint from whose holy life they might learn so much.

There in her mountain home bright roses and forget-me-nots—S. Elizabeth's own special flowers—bloom with a strange luxuriance; seeming as though nature would even give to her now, the reverence and the love which is denied her by men.

CHAPTER XXII.

Something about those S. Elizabeth left behind her.

The story of the life which we have followed in all its joys and sorrows for twenty-four years is told ; there is nought more to say, except to hope that these simple pages have not been written in vain, but that some of those who read them, and upon whom God may have been pleased to lay His chastening Hand in very love, may seek strength where S. Elizabeth sought and found it—even in the Sacred Heart of Jesus. And to those whose lines have fallen in pleasant places, to whom God has given all His good gifts, and into whose life no great sorrow has yet fallen, the story of S. Elizabeth also speaks ; for it tells them so to think of Jesus's sufferings amid their joy, that when trouble does come to them, (as it does unto the life of all of us,) like her they may ask Him to be with them in the dark days, of Whom they were ever mindful when the sun shone most brightly.

A few words about those whom the Saint left on earth to mourn her loss, and whom she influenced by her holy example, may not be out of place here. When the news of his daughter's death reached King

Andrew of Hungary, he gave way to violent grief, and reproached himself for not having sufficiently honoured and appreciated her during her life, and not done half enough for one who was so good and holy. But ere he died he had the comfort of seeing S. Elizabeth's sanctity recognised by the Church; a few months after her canonisation he was taken to his rest, to be with her he had loved so well in the Kingdom that was not of earth. In 1238 the old Duchess Sophia was called to her last account; but she too had, as we have seen, been allowed to witness that solemn scene in the Church at Marburg, when crowned heads bowed low before the corpse of her, who on earth had led the life of voluntary poverty, and when the Church's hymns had mingled with the simple name of Elizabeth the word She puts into the mouths of her children in token of praise, Alleluia! Alleluia! Those little ones, in whom Elizabeth's loving heart had been so bound up, were one and all worthy of their mother. Their greatest boast ever was that they were *her* children; and when they signed their names they always affixed the title of which they were so justly proud *sons* and *daughters* of S. Elizabeth. Sophia and Gertrude each died abbesses of the respective convents in which they had humbly and faithfully served their noviciate.

Young Hermann, at the age of sixteen, took possession of his father's dominions, which his uncle Henry had up to this time governed for him. Then he went on a journey to France to serve as a page in the court, as the custom of the age was, before young men were vested with the honour of knighthood. Whilst he was there, Blanche of Castile, the mother of S. Louis, noticed the boy, who was conspicuous amongst his companions by his fair beauty and long golden hair. She asked who he was, and was told that he was the eldest son of S. Elizabeth of Hungary. She went up to him and said: "Fair youth, thou hadst a blessed mother, where did she kiss thee?" The young Duke blushed, and pointed to a place on his forehead between his eyes. The Queen reverently pressed her lips to the spot, and often afterwards repeated the embrace; and thus the mother of a Saint honoured with touching devotion the son of a Saint.

The young and virtuous Prince of Thuringia married Helena, the daughter of Otho Duke of Brunswick. A long and honourable career seemed to be open to him, but he died in 1241 at the early age of sixteen; and it is said that his death was caused by poison administered by order of his uncle the Landgrave Henry. On his deathbed he asked that he might be buried by the side of his sainted mother; but the cruel Henry would not even grant this request, and young Hermann was laid in the Chapel of Reinhartsbrunn, in the tomb of his royal father.

Henry, now the sole inheritor of the broad lands of Thuringia, was proclaimed king of the Romans in

1246, the Pope (Innocent IV.) having excommunicated Frederick II. for his opposition to the rights and privileges of the Church. But Henry's power was of short duration; he died in 1248, and, although he had been married three times, he left no children. And in this judgment of God, the faithful saw the just punishment of his perfidy towards S. Elizabeth, and of that terrible crime of which he had been guilty towards her son. Perhaps at the last he may have repented of the many sins of his life, for his last request was that he might be buried in the Dominican Convent at Eisenach, which he had founded in expiation of the evil he had done to his sister-in-law.

Duke Conrad during his early life had given himself up to every kind of dissipation, but at last God called him to repentance, and we have already seen how he laboured for the canonisation of S. Elizabeth. He became grand master of the Teutonic knights, and his piety, justice, and modesty made him the brightest ornament of that Order. He lived a life of great self-denial, and did public penance for all the wrong he had done. He died in 1243, and his tomb is still to be seen in the Church at Marburg, the first stone of which he had laid in honour of his sister-in-law.

Thuringia was now distracted by civil war. S. Elizabeth's eldest daughter, Sophia, who had married the Duke of Brabant, claimed the sovereignty for herself and her little son. Bravely and nobly she fought

for the inheritance of her fathers, but she was obliged
to forego her claim to Thuringia, whilst she was
allowed to retain the rule of Hesse, which has descended
in a direct line to the posterity of S. Elizabeth of
Hungary to this day. Sophia died in 1284, at the age
of sixty, after a life spent in watching with tender care
over her family and her dominions. She too sleeps in
the church at Marburg, sacred to the memory of her
mother.

And now it only remains for us to speak of him who
perhaps more than all others helped to make S.
Elizabeth all that we have seen her during the last
days of her life, helped her to give up the last remnants
of self-will which still clung to her, and to bear all the
indignities he chose to lay upon her on earth, so that
her reward in heaven might be greater, her crown
brighter and more radiant. Conrad of Marburg was
called to his rest on the 30th of July, 1233, as he was
travelling from Mayence to Marburg.

That same impetuosity which had ever been his
chief characteristic was the immediate cause of his
death. On his journey he was surprised by several
knights and vassals of the Count of Sayn, whom,
in his excessive zeal for the faith, he had denounced
for heresy. A good Franciscan monk was his sole
attendant, and when the knights attacked Maître
Conrad, he put his arm round him in order to defend
him from the cowardly blows which were falling fast

and thick upon him.   But their adversaries were too
strong for them ; both priests were killed, praising
God to the last that they had been allowed to die
for the faith of the Church.

Maître Conrad's body was buried in the chapel of
the hospital of his native town, near the tomb of the
gentle lady whose true interests, in spite of much that
may be censured in his conduct, ever lay very near his
heart.

LONDON :
SWIFT AND CO., REGENT PRESS, KING STREET,
REGENT STREET, W.

Made in the USA
San Bernardino, CA
28 April 2017